THE ART OF
DREAMING
SMALL

*Live Your Bucket List Now and
Make Every Day Count*

Mare Rosenbaum, CPCC

BALBOA.
PRESS
A DIVISION OF HAY HOUSE

Balboa Press books may be ordered through booksellers or by contacting:

Balboa Press
A Division of Hay House
1663 Liberty Drive
Bloomington, IN 47403
www.balboapress.com
1 (877) 407-4847

Because of the dynamic nature of the Internet, any web addresses or links contained in this book may have changed since publication and may no longer be valid. The views expressed in this work are solely those of the author and do not necessarily reflect the views of the publisher, and the publisher hereby disclaims any responsibility for them.

The author of this book does not dispense medical advice or prescribe the use of any technique as a form of treatment for physical, emotional, or medical problems without the advice of a physician, either directly or indirectly. The intent of the author is only to offer information of a general nature to help you in your quest for emotional and spiritual well-being. In the event you use any of the information in this book for yourself, which is your constitutional right, the author and the publisher assume no responsibility for your actions.

Any people depicted in stock imagery provided by Getty Images are models, and such images are being used for illustrative purposes only. Certain stock imagery © Getty Images.

Print information available on the last page.

ISBN: 978-1-9822-1536-1 (sc)
ISBN: 978-1-9822-1538-5 (hc)
ISBN: 978-1-9822-1537-8 (e)

Library of Congress Control Number: 2018913018

Balboa Press rev. date: 11/14/2018

"*The Art of Dreaming Small provides a path for introspection that exercises the mind, body and spirit. Rosenbaum applies her own life experience to her prescribed practice and the results are truly inspiring.*"

— Mary Brunet

"*Even though I wasn't even thinking about making a bucket list, I've already gone to the office supply store to buy large pieces of paper because I can't wait to get started on the process of living small, medium, and large right away!*"

— Lisa Krueger-Gavin

"*I have enjoyed this book SO MUCH. I wish I had had it at various times in my life when I was trying to make a change or a decision, or push myself to a new level.*"

— Helen B., 83

Dedication

To Mom, the Danish farm girl from Hempstead, NY who taught me pragmatism (e.g., "diamonds are lovely, but you can't eat 'em!"); to Dad, the brigadier general who gave me the odd-couple gifts of strategy and dreaming—thank you for showing me that work is play.

Contents

Acknowledgements

First and foremost, to Jan who loves everything I do, and sees me completely. Thank you for selflessly helping me "take the hill." Without even trying, you make every day a "10."

To my gorgeous daughters, Cecily (the lioness who I'm certain will save the free world all while looking like Audrey Hepburn) and Eva (whose beauty is exceeded only by her wit and intelligence). Thank you for so generously reading this book and for kindly (courageously!) giving me critical feedback.

To my beautiful sons Alec (my tech guru whose mischievous humor makes my heart smile) and Matthew (who has no idea the gifts he possesses, among them, he writes like he breathes). Thank you both for listening to my adventures, taking me seriously, and talking "shop."

To my siblings Jeanne and Paul, first, thanks for letting me use your names without having read this book, (now that's trust); for showing me what dreaming large and small looks like; and whose persistence toward both I so admire.

To my fellow travelers, whose unconditional love gave me my voice.

To the lovely Cranes, my certification pod mates (especially CPL, Leonid!), whose loving support and expert coaching showed me how.

To my clients who allow me to fulfill my calling.

To Peggy, Nancy, and Donna, the wisest, most lovingly truthful women I know.

To Lisa who can always make me laugh, who has listened endlessly to these adventure stories, and whose friendship I treasure.

To Turie, just because.

Author's Note

While these are true stories of real people, I've changed the names and identifying details to protect their privacy, especially because my friends and clients had no idea (nor did I) that they would end up in a book. Any resulting resemblances to persons living or dead are entirely coincidental and unintentional. *The Art of Dreaming Small* is a work of nonfiction. All stories and conversations are recounted as they happened, subject to the limitations of memory.

Introduction
The Eighth Wonder

Sifnos. Ever hear of it? Me neither. We are on our way there now, on a ferry that boarded before dawn, heading to a small island in Greece. Last night was a "10," you know, a never-forget-it-as-long-as-you-live experience. After arriving from Amsterdam where had met a friend for a day at the beach, then saw local artists' drawings from the early 1800's at the oldest museum in Holland, we walked the streets below the Parthenon. I'm not kidding.

How did it happen? I am wondering myself. Several unforeseen events occurred: finding a new friend, with whom I connected through relocation work; Jan, my partner, and I created our bucket list; and, airfare suddenly dropped. In two days, we will be witness to my new friend's wedding. Serendipitous? Maybe. All I know is that we wrote "Mediterranean" in the category of "blue water" about six months ago and here we are. The dream became *real*. Yes, it cost money and required difficult choices, but we knew exactly what we were aiming for, and that is the power of creating a bucket list. Without a firm values-based desire in front of us every day, this would have gone into the realm of someday.

Today, we will arrive at our boutique hotel, a white nest of comfort decorated with billowing turquoise, blue, and white linen curtains atop a cliff that overlooks the Aegean Sea. Tonight, we will toast our hosts under the stars at a beachside cafe; and tomorrow we will witness two, once-in-a-lifetime occasions: the christening of my friend's son, and her wedding. I will stand firmly to witness their love, and breathe deeply as witness to this extraordinary moment. Extraordinary is the only word that comes to mind, and only possible because we, Jan and I, named our intention by creating our bucket list, but the key, I think, was starting small.

One thing I'm learning through my coaching is that hearts have no borders. The things that people live and die for are not only the same anywhere, but they're small, everyday things. My coaching colleagues are from Russia, Spain, England, Canada, Brazil, California, Sweden, Aruba, and Argentina. We could not be more culturally different; we could not be more intrinsically the same. For this reason, I encourage you to dream bigger dreams too— to see the world, and to experience others as fully as humanly possible.

There's magic in this. I don't know how it happens, I don't know if it will also happen for you, but since creating our bucket list we have experienced extraordinary things that can be attained through goal setting and hard work, but there seems to be a serendipitous quality to how opportunities that "help you" appear. Other people have written about this phenomenon at length and I know why. When magic happens it's so phenomenal that you just have to share it. I wish I had a fail-safe prescription for how to get this magic to happen for you too. *The Art of Dreaming Small* is my attempt.

Eat, Pray, Love by Elizabeth Gilbert is one of my favorite books of all time. Liz hates the term "bucket list," yet ironically, she caused a bucket-list sensation when she inspired us by living large and writing about what breathed life back into her battered soul. While most of us experience some form of heartbreak or personal trauma, it's the crisis of living without meaning that is snuffing the light out of us. Living extraordinarily, purposefully, intentionally is what we all long for, but most of us never took our fantasies seriously until she wrote of her magnificent journey.

To put it plainly, she did bucket list-worthy stuff. But how did she know what she wanted to do? This is the kind of thing that bucket list articles, blogs, and websites seem to keep a mystery. For my clients, I needed to unravel it. Liz pulled three, large-category items out of thin air. What if she had been disappointed and returned broke, alone, and jobless? I get that the adventure, the *not knowing*, was part of the lure, but the big, scary, what-if's keep most of us unable to take this sort of risk. What if we could take smaller risks, or understood which risks were worthy enough to take?

Wondering how she arrived at her Italy, India, Indonesia list, I had to go back and look. Remember that scene at the beginning where she's on the bathroom floor, praying? (Like, how could we ever forget?!) It left her with a clue, a beautiful spark of curiosity about God that inspired her to connect to a missing piece of her soul. She began doing meditation, found a guru and the rest is history. That was India. She followed her pull toward Italy by learning Italian and feeling what it was like to speak it. "Every word was like a singing sparrow, a magic trick, a truffle for me." How compelling. (That would get me to Italy.) Then there's Indonesia. Liz gets a "10-minute palm reading" by a "demented Balinese medicine man" (in New York I'm assuming). That's about a $20 adventure i.e., small. How did she know with such certainty that Bali should be a place where she wanted to live for three to four months? That's big. Something ignited her imagination, and I'm guessing that several other values that were unconscious, took root and the imperative to go felt real and solid. In each instance, there's a tiny spark that shines at the surface of a value that lies hidden below. That's what I want to unearth in you. I want you to find your sparks.

This is going to sound like magic, but there's a method to it. I'm writing this six months and six days after creating our bucket list, and I'm noticing that most of what we wrote is already checked off or is in the process of coming about. That's crazy. I know what you're thinking: "You probably haven't reached very high, you made it too easy." Make it easy. Please do. This method is designed to get you started in a can-do-it-today kind of way. But throw in some far off, wild ideas too. Those happen.

Here's the method, at least part of it: built into your final list are small, medium, and large categories. The purpose is not only to test your ideas before you sink time, money and effort into them, but also to create energetic momentum. The book, *The Secret,* talks about actually feeling how you'll feel when you have what you want. They give the example of closing your eyes, imagining gripping the wheel of your new Ferrari, and feeling the excitement of driving it. With *The Art of Dreaming Small*, you don't have to imagine; you actually sample the experience in a smaller way. When I created my bucket list I wanted to feel and experience something I value NOW. I didn't want to wait. As it turns out, sampling a smaller version may have a significant impact on your ability to imagine and therefore "manifest" your bigger items. I do want to be cautious here with the word "manifest," the over-used, over-promising word of our time. To me, it implies having something unattainable fall out of the sky and into your life. That is magical thinking. That's not what I'm saying. The manifestation I'm talking about is in identifying what is most important to you, planning and working to attain those experiences, then feeling fulfillment as things you didn't dare imagine before start happening regularly, at times serendipitously. That's magic.

So, here's an example of how some of these experiences played out for me (Jan and I combined our list therefore some items are specific to me and some are specific to him in the IDEA REALIZATION values section): on our list, I wrote in the "Large" category of the value expression "invention," that I would "write a book." I didn't know what my book would be, and I had been talking about this for at least a decade so I knew that writing a book belonged in the Large category. It would be a big deal for me. I thought that a workshop might end up being a part of it (written in the "Small" category of that same value expression— you'll understand how this works later).

When I started developing this bucket list method, I simply started to take notes on how I was doing this for my clients so that I could repeat it. About a month later, as we started to experience some of the items on our list I decided to journal about how those experiences were coming about. The note-taking on the process combined with the journaling became this book.

Back to the Small category: the idea of the book, in turn, gave me the idea for a three-day workshop. I tried to figure out where I could give a three-day workshop inexpensively and I kept hitting a dead end. The cost of the space for three full days (how long I thought it needed to be) would be significant, and the time commitment for people including possible travel would be significant as well. How would I market this? How much would it cost me to fill seats? Overwhelmed, I set it aside. A couple of days later I remembered taking continuing education classes at a local high school. They offered all kinds of classes, some for credits, but some purely for the sake of learning. I contacted the continuing education organization and submitted my application to teach a three-evening class on developing your bucket list. At the end of this month, I'll be giving this "workshop."

Additionally, an actual workshop came about: a colleague from a completely unrelated field said that a friend of hers was putting together a book festival and was looking for people to teach a workshop for writers. *Presto-magico*. There it was again. She connected me to her friend, I sent her my bio, interviewed, and in two weeks I'll be giving a workshop to about a hundred writers at a book festival.

To recap: The Large item, writing this book, developed through the course of working on these other projects and with my coaching clients, yet it had eluded me for a decade. Now it was made clear and totally doable; the Small item, the workshop, came about two ways: one I developed, the other dropped out of the sky.

Chalking it up to luck? Okay, let me tell you about this one. I wrote "Project Home Philly" in the Small category to get involved in some way with that specific local organization for the homeless. In the Large section of that same value expression I wrote "create a self-sufficient village." I often fantasized about building a village of tiny houses as community. Tiny houses have been a fascination of mine for years. My idea was to create a self-sufficient village of tiny houses for homeless families. Still thinking "Small," I searched the Project Home Philly website to volunteer. There was nothing available that fit my experience. Disappointed, I let it go. In the meantime, an associate referred a neighbor to me for coaching. He's an entrepreneur who has multiple projects going on. One of those, my new client enthusiastically explained, is that he saved a non-profit from dissolving; they have been serving the *homeless* for over 35 years. He continued about the project. Essential to saving the organization, this project involves building a cooperative community using tiny houses that face onto a common area. Explaining excitedly, he told me that what will make this village so unique is that they each pitch in to do work for their common good. They will have a garden, a common kitchen, a common recreation area. He will be building a *self-sufficient village with tiny houses.* As part of our coaching relationship I would be coaching him through that project and its obstacles. Magic once again: I get to contribute, albeit indirectly, in the building of a self-sufficient village for homeless single parents. I never could have predicted that such a far-off dream of mine would come to fruition in this way. There are so many other bucket list dreams that are coming true that I believe that before the year is out, we'll have to create another list. This may become our New Year's tradition.

Finally, for all the wonderful places we've gone, and all the fulfilling things we do, it's people that make the experience a "10." Be sure to include others.

Discovering how to create the experiences in life that we value is one thing, but the feeling that we are working with something unseen, some kind of organizing energy, feels to me like we (I'm not the only one) are discovering the Eighth Wonder of the World. Whatever it is, creating your bucket list with this method seems to call it into action.

I sincerely desire this for you: that you too will discover Eighth-Wonder magic through the creation of your own bucket list. Moreover, I wish you the kind of fulfillment and satisfaction you long for, the kind that I've experienced that comes from living your values, dreaming small and living large. Let's begin, shall we?

CHAPTER ONE
You Want What?!

What does it mean when two clients at the same time, thousands of miles apart, come to you to help them write their bucket list? What are the chances? A believer in the Law of Attraction[1], I wondered if I was going to find out that I had a terminal illness.

One of these clients was at the top of his game, in his forties, a vice president of a multi-million-dollar international company. The other was barely a senior, healthy, adventurous, financially independent, and capable of doing anything she desired. My mind was saying, *what in the hell are you talking about? Why are you thinking about the END of your life when you're just about to live it? What stops either of you from doing anything you want to do?*

What came out of my mouth (as a newly minted coach) was, "Tell me more."

---

[1] In case you're wondering what the Law of Attraction is, Wikipedia explains it this way: "In the New Thought philosophy, the Law of Attraction is the belief that by focusing on positive or negative thoughts, people can bring positive or negative experiences into their life. The belief is based on the idea that people and their thoughts are both made from "pure energy," and that through the process of "like energy attracting like energy" a person can improve their own health, wealth, and personal relationships."

Jeanne, client number one—a true empath, could sense my discomfort with what sounded like a death knell. Reversing roles, she assured me that creating a bucket list was *positive*. To her it was a way of living intentionally. "I don't want to get to the end of my life and realize I haven't lived it." She went on to explain, "I think I have a good ten years before I have to worry about my health limitations. I want to use that time wisely."

Paul, client number two, explained, "Every day I go through the motions, I do the same thing, I'm tied to my cell phone, work is 24/7, I go to the gym, I come home, but this isn't living." He went on. "There's always traffic, some horrible story in the news, shootings, people don't care about each other . . . they don't care that they're destroying the environment . . . they're always on their cell phones, and I do it too. My brother barely talks to me, and I never actually *take the time* to enjoy life. Friends, and family . . . enjoyment, isn't that what life's about? Why does no one do this? I'm tired of it. I don't want that to be me anymore."

This sounded like the lament of our time. I hear this often, in every setting.

With both clients, when there are few limitations on what exciting and wonderful things they could do, where would I begin to help them create a bucket list that truly mattered? And, what if they spent time and money doing something fantastical that turned out to be meh? As far as end of life: they may have ten years, or twenty, or two days, who knows? What about living now?

I longed for them each to experience joy; to experience intimate connection. I longed for their contentment. I sensed their frustration and restlessness. Both are caring, kind, loving people who want meaning. Together, we would soul search and learn what compels them, what loving every day means. To guide them in this process, I would do this for myself first. Every weekend I would work, just one step ahead of them, not knowing where it would end up.

From *The Secret*, to *Think and Grow Rich*, to vision boards, many of us have attempted to call into our lives our dreams and greatest fantasies. For some, it works. For the rest of us, well, it seems too out of reach. I've tried both methods to no avail. I believe there is power, maybe something energetic or magnetic to naming and claiming what you desire. So why doesn't it work? Perhaps I'm too impatient, and my clients needed something now, today, not someday. Paul will never do visioning every day. To take a purely coaching approach, I could help him set goals, take steps to achieve them, work through his own resistance or other obstacles and increase his motivation, but, what's the goal?

Even in my coaching classes, I have to admit, that the visioning exercises we did to discover our life purpose resulted in nothing for me. It felt forced. Where does purpose reside within each of us? What's the path to discovering it? How would I wrestle this awesome task (awesome in the truest sense) into submission? It may happen that we find our way, but how would I repeat it successfully with every client? To feel fulfilled when the experience has nothing to do with work, to live our purpose outside of career, unless it's volunteerism, feels at times even more elusive. Any purpose exploration I've seen or done has to do with what we do in the world of work, but what about finding meaningful enjoyment? Experience for our own sake seems contradictory to purpose. Like an explorer, I set out to discover unknown territory.

We all owe it to ourselves to live well, and if we believe in a Higher Power, God, or The Universe, we feel indebted to have been given the precious gift of life. How do we honor that?

Is it enough to honor ourselves? Elizabeth Gilbert's year-long sojourn in *Eat, Pray, Love* is all about honoring herself: satisfying desires, curiosity about herself/others/the world, spirituality. It's about finding her own, highly personal connection with the divine, but here's what's interesting to me: simply living from her personal divine connection is what seems to be so fulfilling for her. Perhaps one lesson for us is that translating our very personal experience of our Higher Power, whatever that is to us, seems to bring us joy, and yes, purpose. Given that, it seems that the most important place to begin would be inside of us, with our spiritual connection.

This will never work for Paul, he's atheist. I think the idea of connecting to his divinity will turn him off totally. Perhaps for him this deep connection can be to himself. What does he feel strongly about? What inspires the best in him? What connects him to his excitement, joy, pleasure, others? What does he care about so deeply that he cannot tolerate its opposite?

Many people find great satisfaction in giving to or being part of a cause. Whenever I think of nonprofit work, I think of self-sacrifice through volunteerism. That won't work for Paul either. It may work for Jeanne though. Another author takes the approach that finding your purpose in a cause can serve you as well, and that we should look for a win/win. The book is called, *A Selfish Plan to Change the World: Finding Big Purpose in Big Problems,* written by Justin Dillon. He takes a cannot-tolerate approach to help you discover your purpose, or in his words, "your riot." Here's how he connects "riot" to purpose:

FINDING YOUR RIOT

"You might be thinking the word riot is a little over-the-top. It sounds scary and violent, so why would anyone want to find one? Riot conjures images of violent clashes in the streets with a mob launching Molotov cocktails on one side and police in gas masks on the other. I understand the word riot sounds downright dangerous and perhaps unlawful. I've been around a few riots, and they are definitely chaotic. The riot inside you doesn't look like any of these images. Your riot isn't violent or destructive, but it does have one thing in common with traditional riots: Your riot is a place inside of you where you stand up and say that something is wrong. It's where you turn your indignation into action. Simply put, finding your riot is how you find your purpose."

Justin Dillon found his riot while standing in a recording studio lobby, reading the cover of a newspaper article in a paper that happened to be sitting on a coffee table. It ignited such a strong reaction in him he felt he had to do something about it. The rest of his life, his work, all of his experience, skill, and business connections came to the fore to support his new mission: eradicating human trafficking and child slavery. His newfound purpose is powerful, life-changing for himself and others, and there is no doubt of the worthiness of pursuing it. It led him to far-reaching corners of the world to make movies, give concerts, and enjoy many other bucket-list worthy experiences. It makes a great story, however I have the feeling this isn't what my clients are after.

In exploring ideas for my own bucket list, I wondered if "finding my riot" is me. It feels inspirational. Before I consider seriously pursuing such an all-consuming mission, I need to remember that every time I watch John Oliver's *Last Week Tonight* I pick up a new cause that I'm on fire to do something about. I had to stop watching. This could be a danger zone for you too. It would be easy to get so sidetracked into a cause—let's face it, they're all worthy—that it becomes dissociative.[2] What I want my clients to do, and for you to do, is to honor yourself not lose yourself, an important distinction. My clients want to live within the lives they've created, only more meaningfully. Going overboard (doing something crazy), or wishful thinking is not what this book is about.

The method I'm about to walk you through is grounded in positive psychology[3], bona fide coaching practices[4], my years of work with relocating Fortune 500 executives, and facilitating businesses with strategic planning and innovation.

May this book lead you to discover more about yourself, to find fulfillment and joy within your life, and at every opportunity.

---

[2] The dictionary definition of dissociate is "to sever association of oneself; separate." www.dictionary.com

[3] **Positive psychology** is "the scientific study of what makes life most worth living," or "the scientific study of positive human functioning and flourishing on multiple levels that include the biological, personal, relational, institutional, cultural, and global dimensions of life." Positive psychology is concerned with "the good life," reflection about what holds the greatest value in life – the factors that contribute the most to a well-lived and fulfilling life. Wikipedia. For more information, please visit: https://ppc.sas.upenn.edu/people/martin-ep-seligman

[4] The Co-Active Coach˙ Training program is the only coach training program based on the Co-Active Model, a tried-and-true approach that provides a powerful process for engaging with others and is supported by current scientific research. The creators of this model, Coaches Training Institute (CTI) is an Industry Leader whose founders were among the initial pioneers of the coaching profession. Over the last 25 years, CTI has trained over 55,000 Co-Active coaches worldwide. https://coactive.com/why-cti

CHAPTER TWO
It (Actually) Happened

It was a cold, boring weekend in February when Jan and I sat in bed, pen in hand. "I have a hunch. I want to try this. You game?" I said. Jan has a strong analytical mind, he's a logical thinker, and very pragmatic. Oddly, he is also able and willing to "vision" easily. Running only slightly ahead of my clients, I had to try what I thought would work for them. I wasn't willing to make them the guinea pigs. Why not try this out ourselves? And, what if it works? Creating our own bucket list was very appealing. Complicating things, I had a combination of methods in mind that I thought might work. We could discover where my method falls short, take some wrong turns, test it. Mulling it over in my mind for the past several weeks, I was convinced that there would be more to this than simply naming values. How would I make these values come to life? How would we know what to rule out until we explored each one exhaustively?

Jan, an unwitting participant to a much bigger commitment, said enthusiastically, "Sure!"

We began. I asked him to recall a peak experience from his childhood— anything at all— then see it vividly in his mind and describe it to me.

"I'm about five years old, sitting on the patio floor of my grandparent's house in Switzerland playing with Legos," he said. I waited in silence, while he explored the scene unfolding for him. "Not a care in the world. I am building a house."

"What's special about that?" I asked.

"I'm making it real from an idea in my mind — no rules, completely free to create whatever is in my mind . . ." I let a few seconds pass, managing my urge to know more. "It's warm outside, the house is beautiful, marble floors and a fireplace. A view of the lake and village, and the mountain that looks like an old lady with very bad teeth." I tried hard not to chuckle. The things he notices...

And so, it went for two more peak experiences. Having learned about levels of listening in coaching, I was able to discern several values from Jan's memories. Briefly, Level One Listening helps you to be aware of your own feelings, inference, and assumptions. Being aware of what is going on in your own head frees you from it. Level Two Listening gives you the specifics of the story, words someone uses and context like what is happening and when. Level Three Listening however, gives you the important stuff, the meaning behind the story, as with Jan's feelings and perceptions.

I must admit, it took a little self-management (Level One) to get past the fact that he had grown up going to his grandparents' house in Switzerland. In my head I was hearing, *Yeah, and I grew up going to my grandparents' two-bedroom, dark, dirty, overcrowded house in Valley Stream, NY!* Ah, the challenge of working with your intimate partner. Thanks to my training, I was able to quiet that mental noise to listen to what was truly dear to him about that memory. What I heard when I tuned into Level Three Listening, was CREATIVITY (from his fond memory of creative play with Legos); IDEA REALIZATION (imagining the house and making it real); and, BEAUTY (the fact that a 5-year-old would even notice the fireplace and marble floors was really striking to me.) *That is so Jan.* And so, it went.

This brings me to an important point: you will need a partner for this exercise and other exercises to come. In fact, this whole art-of-dreaming-small method requires a partner, someone who will either help you with your bucket list (like a friend), or someone who wants to create their own. It isn't easy to do this with your intimate partner and I wouldn't recommend it unless you have a very open, accepting relationship with mutual respect and no judgement. It worked for us because my training helped me get out of Level One, and I admit, our relationship is extraordinary. Keep the idea of working with a partner in the back of your mind until you're ready to begin; someone will want to support you.

Next, I demonstrated to Jan the three levels of listening and asked him to listen to my peak experience memories. Thankfully, he's a quick study. He waited until I found a memory that I wanted to explore. "I am eight or nine-years old, in my backyard. Chairs are set up for the audience, and a clothesline is stretched clear across the yard with sheets pinned to it. I created a play, complete with commercials, and we had invited the neighborhood families to our performance." I could feel the excitement again.

"You did what?!" was his un-coach-like response. Pushing past wanting to come out of this memory and explain it, I stayed with exploring what was exciting about it to me and answered his question.

"The fun of figuring out how to stage it, and who did what, and how each kid could contribute, making invitations and tickets . . . ." I was astonished at how much detail I could remember when I pictured it in my mind. I could even feel the humidity of that summer morning, the jitters of not knowing if anyone would show up, staring hopefully at the rickety wooden gate where our audience would enter, feeling the butterflies of not knowing if we would flop. The amazement and joy of seeing each person file in and take a seat was palpable. I reported, "We actually made $40! I was so excited to actually make this kind of money. It felt like a big deal." Of course, I didn't include the part where we show the money to my friend's mom and she swiftly removes the cash from my hand, all the while smiling with confidence that she knows best, and declares, "A charity will be very happy for this contribution!" A psychologist would have a field day with this.

Back to our values exploration, the values Jan heard were: MAKING IT REAL (having an idea and working at it until it becomes real which would later match his value becoming IDEA REALIZATION); STRATEGIZING (having a vision and figuring out how to carry it out); CREATIVITY (writing the play and the commercials); RECOGNITION (making money).

This continued for both of us until we each had a list of values. Rather than create separate bucket lists, we decided that because we do nearly everything together, and that it would be fun to test this together, we would create one bucket list that represented both of us. Neither STRATEGIZING nor CREATIVITY would make it to our combined list which is fine. There were plenty of values we had in common. Now we had something to work with!

We continued the next day, putting big post-it sheets on the wall, gathering our colored markers and scribbling out ideas. Brainstorming. Narrowing. Taking wrong turns. Starting over. After three hours, we were exhausted. We had hit a dead end.

Over the next several days it was all we could talk about. We prioritized, we made another couple of attempts, when finally, it all came together. As a facilitator for companies in need of strategies and innovative ideas I know how this goes. In a professional situation, I know where we want to end up, what it will look like, and what they'll do with the ideas they generate. With this bucket list method, neither of us knew what the end product would look like or how it would work. Still unsure if our bucket list was actually doable, or if it would create true peak experiences, we posted it on the wall of our bedroom.

We didn't think to look at it every day, though I noticed that when we were presented with an opportunity we would check the opportunity against our shared values. If we could check off all six, we would make it happen no matter what. If the opportunity only agreed with one or two values, we would put less time, effort, and money toward it. This list turned out to be a practical tool, even for work projects we were considering. We now had a compass to gage what we would do, when, and how.

When about six weeks went by we looked it over carefully because it seemed that we were doing extraordinary things and having fabulous weekends. To our surprise, even only six weeks in, opportunities seemed to materialize out of thin air and we were ticking off bigger items than we thought we would for years.

Here's how that Greek isle trip actually happened:

On our list we had written the word "Mediterranean" in our Large experience column as an expression of several values combining "blue water," "exotic location," and "adventure." We had decided to give a name to someplace we would like to visit together.

Separately, I had heard a colleague lament that she was very unhappy where she was living in France, and how guilty she felt about asking her husband to move again. Adding to her guilt was the thought of disrupting her children's education, including their newly-acquired language.

Having extensive experience in coaching executive families through relocation, I reached out to her privately to offer assistance. I began by helping her to emotionally embrace 'what is', and empowering her to approach her husband for a conversation about her needs. Then I asked them to brainstorm a list of places to consider. Here was their list: Amsterdam, The Hague, London, Barcelona, Stockholm, Copenhagen, Geneva, Munich, and Milan. After working with them to identify what they valued and what their requirements were specific to the stage of life they're in, they compared their choices and narrowed it to three cities to begin more detailed research. Before long they had a plan that honored everyone's values, needs and priorities. My colleague and her husband were so grateful they invited us to their wedding on a little island *in Greece*. I knew she and her partner were Greek, however I had no idea they had plans for a wedding, nor could I have ever imagined we would be invited. Looking over our list a few days later we saw the word Mediterranean, then referred to our earlier brainstorming sheets and found the word "Greece."

Since then we've checked off at least a half dozen other items on our bucket list and agreed, if this is how "it" happens, let's think bigger. We got out the markers and began adding ideas. Now we're dating them to know what we added, when. This list has a life of its own and what we love about it is that, unlike your typical bucket list, there is never an end. What we've created, and what you will also create, is a place to begin. I'm certain that by the time I finish writing this book, several more bucket list ideas of ours will come to fruition. I'll be sure to let you know in the last chapter. Try not to skip ahead!

CHAPTER THREE
What's Important

To truly hear another, hear what their words are saying, and *everything they're not saying,* is a gift to them. It happens so rarely in our get-it-done world, that it actually takes conscious effort and practice.

My first session with Jeanne began. "Close your eyes and scan your childhood for a peak experience, something you feel good about even now as you recall it." Jeanne is prone to over thinking so I added, "there is no right or wrong, there is no 'best', there is only joyful feeling." Sometimes it's easier to find the feeling first, then let the images emerge. I knew this might take time. "Let's just sit quietly until one comes to mind." Aware that she may be feeling on stage while I sat staring at her, I added, "I'll close my eyes too." This also helped me concentrate on what she was saying.

After several minutes her voice emerged in a flat, almost hypnotic tone. "Well, I don't know if this is right, or if I'm remembering it correctly, and it seems inconsequential, just a fragment." Jeanne had a rough childhood. I imagined that finding a joyful memory would be difficult. Therapy and twelve-step programs focus on inventorying past trauma and connecting it to today's behavior, triggers, then recovery from reactive emotions and behaviors (e.g., before recovery I did *that*, now I do *this*). I know she's done years of that kind of work making it easier to recall traumatic memories, but we've got to find one positive memory, just one.

"I'm eating latkes" she said. Silence.

Though relieved, I managed to not say, *Oh good!* What I did ask after a few eternally long seconds passed was, "What else?"

"I'm at the kitchen table." More silence followed with steady shallow breathing. I could tell she was concentrating really hard.

"Who's there?"

Responding as though this should be obvious to me, she blurted, "My grandfather! He's making the latkes."

"How old are you?"

"I'm not sure, maybe ten? Maybe eight?"

"Smell the latkes cooking, see the table . . . feel the contentment. (I was taking a stab in hope of stirring up more details, and if I was wrong, I knew she would correct me.) Jeanne's words are measured. Each one is very important to her. When she speaks, she is extremely articulate.

I prodded. "What's important about this?"

"Everything's good, I'm safe . . . Safety."

"Why latkes? What do latkes mean?"

"It's just something he knew I liked, and always made them for me." (I'm glad I didn't assume it was a holiday. That would have taken us down a different path.)

"What does the room look like?"

"Well, it's small. The table is wooden. There are windows . . . and it's raining." She continued softly, "I love the rain." Jeanne was on a roll, and maybe this would lead to a different memory. It didn't matter, only finding peak experiences mattered. The more the better.

"In fact, I'm sitting outside on the curb in the street between our house and the neighbors, just letting the rain fall on me. Just letting it fall. I liked to play in the rain." Her brows furrowed then suddenly raised. "It's only raining on one house!" she exclaimed as though she were seeing this for the first time.

"How do you know?" I asked because it seemed odd.

"I can see that just across the street the sun is shining, and that is just AMAZING to me." I could hear the awe and inspiration in her voice. I could hear the excitement of discovery. I opened my eyes to read what else was happening. Her eyelids fluttered excitedly.

"What else do you notice?"

"I like to sit quietly and watch the rain, feel the rain."

"That's great, Jeanne. Is there anything else you notice?"

She answered, "No, that's it. I don't know where anyone else is. It's a happy time."

When you're ready to 'come back' just open your eyes and sit quietly. There's nothing you need to say. Just enjoy the feeling of those two beautiful memories."

While she sat quietly, I jotted down key words. I would check these with her. Even if she would have never said these exact words herself, she'll know if it's true by checking in with her body and seeing if it "feels right" when I say them. In fact, what I witnessed were values and words she didn't actually say such as NATURE (her awe, inspiration and discovery at the rain on one side of the street and feeling the drops fall on her as she played), TRADITION (family, latkes, her routine with her grandfather), and CONNECTION (close "safe" loving relationship).

As it went, these were all values she would agree that she holds deeply. She was astonished. "How did you figure that out?" she was very curious.

I am an intuitive listener and was able to glean this type of information when I would listen to my relocation clients. After coach training, I learned that there's a teachable method for this. Anyone can do it. The secret? I listened in levels, one, two, and three as I had done with Jan.

Here's how it breaks down:

Level One Listening: it's all about what's going on in *my* head. It sounded something like, *this is going to be tough, I hope we don't end up in a trauma memory, latkes, it must be Hanukah, don't make that assumption, get out of your head and get over there with your client!*

Level Two Listening: it's all about what *she's* saying, the exact words, the information. In my mind it sounded something like this: *latkes, grandfather, comfort, food, their routine, home, kitchen age eight or ten, she loves the rain, sitting and letting the rain fall on her, it's raining on her house, but not across the street, it's "just amazing."*

Level Three Listening: it's all about listening to what's being *expressed* yet maybe not being said. It's noticing, feeling, hearing, seeing and sensing. It goes like this: *her energy is lifting in this kitchen; her voice is rising in exclamation about her grandfather. I sense that this routine of theirs is special to her. Her eyelids flutter with excitement. The details are starting to flow. Her pitch is raised, her cadence is more fluid and the tempo picks up. She looks happy, content.*

This is what you will need to pay attention to in order to discern values.

Values. How can such a small word be so perplexing? When you ask someone what their values are, you get a deer-in-the-headlight expression while their brain scrambles both to figure out exactly what the word means, while their saboteurs (I'll explain this in the next chapter) fight every positive thought that pops up. "It's gotta be bigger than that," "values are who you are, idiot," "everybody says *that*," and the thoughts go on, and on. I used to ask this question of my relocating clients. After a lot of silence, resistance, non-answers, self-judgement, fear of each other's judgement or my judgement, a word like "safety" would softly float to the surface. "Great!" I would say to try and encourage more sharing. Think about it though, who on this planet doesn't want to live someplace safe? And so it would go while I chased them around like when you try to pick that one tiny piece of eggshell out of the bowl. You'd think you have it, and just as your spoon reaches the surface, the fragment slips over the edge back into the bowl and off you go again. Let's try to tease out what the value "safety" means because chances are pretty good that it will land on your list. It did with Jeanne.

Safety could be living without fear of crime; freedom to walk alone at night; freedom to walk alone during the day without the homeless approaching you (most common in U.S. cities); that's physical safety. Mostly, my relocating clients look at crime rates, but for which types of crimes? Over how long a period. Is it okay to have very low crime (usually appears green on a crime map) yet have a convicted sexual predator living near your home? Then there's the aspect of safety from natural disasters. If you're coming from New Orleans, San Francisco, the Jersey Shore, or any other area frequently hit with hurricanes, tornadoes, or earthquakes, you may mean physical safety from natural disasters. That's when a value of "safety" means something geographical.

Now we get into a tricky area: socio economics. Many times, my clients would assume an area to be unsafe or high crime because of the way it looks. We would pull into a neighborhood that for some reason signaled to them that it lacked safety. Perhaps the lawns were untrimmed, there might be trash on the street, the shutters were plastic or needed painting, something triggered a gut reaction that felt "unsafe." Likewise, if we pulled into a neighborhood where the gardens looked too trim, too clean, too decorated it could trigger the same feeling, however this time it might be fear of judgement, fear that they could never keep up that appearance. Alarm bells would go off and we were outta there. This is when I learned to ask that cliché coach question, "What does (safety) look like?" That one question alone saved me and my clients tons of time and helped them to understand themselves. It invited discussion and at times debate between the couple. Eventually I realized that a value like "safety" while there are ways to quantify it, is actually subjective. To get a clearer picture in my mind of what safety meant to them, I would ask them if they feel safe where they currently live, look up the statistics there, and get a barometer for comparison. Many times, they were stunned to know that they were living in a statistically higher crime area than they realized. Another great way to understand their value, I would then ask, "What tells you you're safe where you are?" Often what they're really saying is that they feel they belong.

Belonging is an important value. It sounds like, "we know everyone here," "we do a lot together," "there are a lot of teachers, social workers, hospital staff etc. . . ." as they would describe their neighbors, who coincidently, had jobs like theirs. Or, "people here are friendly, they always say hello, ask you how you are, even when we walk into shops. They know us." Even this statement could be teased out with questions like, "How does that feel?" to which they may have many different replies. Their reply would give me more clues possibly pointing to variety, diversity, ethnicity, spirituality etc.

Valuable stuff. This is the gold you're looking for when you listen for someone's values. Mostly, just look for clues, then ask clarifying questions.

Another way to make use of a value like this is to recognize when it's an over-arching value. We'll go into this more later in Chapter Six, but for now, know that some values are so important, that they need to be honored in every value. In the case of "safety," it would mean that if this person doesn't feel safe first and foremost, the other values don't matter. For example, let's say they have a value of "nature," and they have a fear of heights. How safety is honored while in nature would make a go/no go difference. I imagine that this person would not take a hot air balloon ride, or hike the Grand Canyon. In the Small category, it means that they may not enjoy sitting in a city park, if there's the possibility that they might encounter a person or a group of strangers that feel threatening in some way.

To give you something to work with, below is a list of values. It's not exhaustive, and some of them are synonyms. It's long, so don't let it scare you, just take a cursory look, but please don't study it. Listen to your partner first, clarify with questions, and if you don't know what to call it then look at this list. Be sure that you're not doing this the other way around i.e., studying this list then looking to slap a label on what comes up. That would be what I call "outside-in" thinking. Outside-in thinking lends itself to making assumptions. Assumptions are usually wrong. Whenever I've had to start over with someone, or "take a left turn" in the middle of our work together, it's because somewhere along the way I've made a wrong assumption.

The mind loves certainty, and likes to fill in the blanks. We don't usually realize we're doing that until sometime later. Try to remain curious. Curiosity has an innocence and a non-judgmental quality to it. Curiosity ensures that you won't make assumptions and that you'll ask great clarifying questions.

One more thing: remember my description of Level One Listening? Beware of your mind being preoccupied with getting it right. Be over there with your bucket list partner. Another hint is to let them do most of the talking. Let them explore their memory and imagination first without stopping them. Let it flow, that's hard enough (for them). Then when they are finished telling their story, ask clarifying questions. Good luck, and have fun with this! Here's that list I promised you:

[5]Values

1. Abundance
2. Acceptance
3. Accessibility
4. Accomplishment
5. Accountability
6. Accuracy
7. Achievement
8. Acknowledgement
9. Activeness
10. Adaptability
11. Adoration
12. Adroitness
13. Advancement
14. Adventure
15. Affection

---

[5] Credit for this list comes from Steve Pavlina's website, https://www.stevepavlina.com/blog/2004/11/list-of-values/

16. Affluence
17. Aggressiveness
18. Agility
19. Alertness
20. Altruism
21. Amazement
22. Ambition
23. Amusement
24. Anticipation
25. Appreciation
26. Approachability
27. Approval
28. Art
29. Articulacy
30. Artistry
31. Assertiveness
32. Assurance
33. Attentiveness
34. Attractiveness
35. Audacity
36. Availability
37. Awareness
38. Awe
39. Balance
40. Beauty
41. Being the best
42. Belonging
43. Benevolence
44. Bliss
45. Boldness
46. Bravery
47. Brilliance
48. Buoyancy
49. Calmness
50. Camaraderie

51. Candor
52. Capability
53. Care
54. Carefulness
55. Celebrity
56. Certainty
57. Challenge
58. Change
59. Charity
60. Charm
61. Chastity
62. Cheerfulness
63. Clarity
64. Cleanliness
65. Clear-mindedness
66. Cleverness
67. Closeness
68. Comfort
69. Commitment
70. Community
71. Compassion
72. Competence
73. Competition
74. Completion
75. Composure
76. Concentration
77. Confidence
78. Conformity
79. Congruency
80. Connection
81. Consciousness
82. Conservation
83. Consistency
84. Contentment
85. Continuity

86. Contribution
87. Control
88. Conviction
89. Conviviality
90. Coolness
91. Cooperation
92. Cordiality
93. Correctness
94. Country
95. Courage
96. Courtesy
97. Craftiness
98. Creativity
99. Credibility
100. Cunning
101. Curiosity
102. Daring
103. Decisiveness
104. Decorum
105. Deference
106. Delight
107. Dependability
108. Depth
109. Desire
110. Determination
111. Devotion
112. Devoutness
113. Dexterity
114. Dignity
115. Diligence
116. Direction
117. Directness
118. Discipline
119. Discovery
120. Discretion

121. Diversity
122. Dominance
123. Dreaming
124. Drive
125. Duty
126. Dynamism
127. Eagerness
128. Ease
129. Economy
130. Ecstasy
131. Education
132. Effectiveness
133. Efficiency
134. Elation
135. Elegance
136. Empathy
137. Encouragement
138. Endurance
139. Energy
140. Enjoyment
141. Entertainment
142. Enthusiasm
143. Environmentalism
144. Ethics
145. Euphoria
146. Excellence
147. Excitement
148. Exhilaration
149. Expectancy
150. Expediency
151. Experience
152. Expertise
153. Exploration
154. Expressiveness
155. Extravagance

156. Extroversion
157. Exuberance
158. Fairness
159. Faith
160. Fame
161. Family
162. Fascination
163. Fashion
164. Fearlessness
165. Ferocity
166. Fidelity
167. Fierceness
168. Financial independence
169. Firmness
170. Fitness
171. Flexibility
172. Flow
173. Fluency
174. Focus
175. Fortitude
176. Frankness
177. Freedom
178. Friendliness
179. Friendship
180. Frugality
181. Fun
182. Gallantry
183. Generosity
184. Gentility
185. Giving
186. Grace
187. Gratitude
188. Gregariousness
189. Growth
190. Guidance

191. Happiness
192. Harmony
193. Health
194. Heart
195. Helpfulness
196. Heroism
197. Holiness
198. Honesty
199. Honor
200. Hopefulness
201. Hospitality
202. Humility
203. Humor
204. Hygiene
205. Imagination
206. Impact
207. Impartiality
208. Independence
209. Individuality
210. Industry
211. Influence
212. Ingenuity
213. Inquisitiveness
214. Insightfulness
215. Inspiration
216. Integrity
217. Intellect
218. Intelligence
219. Intensity
220. Intimacy
221. Intrepidness
222. Introspection
223. Introversion
224. Intuition
225. Intuitiveness

226. Inventiveness
227. Investing
228. Involvement
229. Joy
230. Judiciousness
231. Justice
232. Keenness
233. Kindness
234. Knowledge
235. Leadership
236. Learning
237. Liberation
238. Liberty
239. Lightness
240. Liveliness
241. Logic
242. Longevity
243. Love
244. Loyalty
245. Majesty
246. Making a difference
247. Marriage
248. Mastery
249. Maturity
250. Meaning
251. Meekness
252. Mellowness
253. Meticulousness
254. Mindfulness
255. Modesty
256. Motivation
257. Mysteriousness
258. Nature
259. Neatness
260. Nerve

261. Noncomformity
262. Obedience
263. Open-mindedness
264. Openness
265. Optimism
266. Order
267. Organization
268. Originality
269. Outdoors
270. Outlandishness
271. Outrageousness
272. Partnership
273. Patience
274. Passion
275. Peace
276. Perceptiveness
277. Perfection
278. Perkiness
279. Perseverance
280. Persistence
281. Persuasiveness
282. Philanthropy
283. Piety
284. Playfulness
285. Pleasantness
286. Pleasure
287. Poise
288. Polish
289. Popularity
290. Potency
291. Power
292. Practicality
293. Pragmatism
294. Precision
295. Preparedness

296. Presence
297. Pride
298. Privacy
299. Proactivity
300. Professionalism
301. Prosperity
302. Prudence
303. Punctuality
304. Purity
305. Rationality
306. Realism
307. Reason
308. Reasonableness
309. Recognition
310. Recreation
311. Refinement
312. Reflection
313. Relaxation
314. Reliability
315. Relief
316. Religiousness
317. Reputation
318. Resilience
319. Resolution
320. Resolve
321. Resourcefulness
322. Respect
323. Responsibility
324. Rest
325. Restraint
326. Reverence
327. Richness
328. Rigor
329. Sacredness
330. Sacrifice

331. Sagacity
332. Saintliness
333. Sanguinity
334. Satisfaction
335. Science
336. Security
337. Self-control
338. Selflessness
339. Self-reliance
340. Self-respect
341. Sensitivity
342. Sensuality
343. Serenity
344. Service
345. Sexiness
346. Sexuality
347. Sharing
348. Shrewdness
349. Significance
350. Silence
351. Silliness
352. Simplicity
353. Sincerity
354. Skillfulness
355. Solidarity
356. Solitude
357. Sophistication
358. Soundness
359. Speed
360. Spirit
361. Spirituality
362. Spontaneity
363. Spunk
364. Stability
365. Status

366. Stealth
367. Stillness
368. Strength
369. Structure
370. Success
371. Support
372. Supremacy
373. Surprise
374. Sympathy
375. Synergy
376. Teaching
377. Teamwork
378. Temperance
379. Thankfulness
380. Thoroughness
381. Thoughtfulness
382. Thrift
383. Tidiness
384. Timeliness
385. Traditionalism
386. Tranquility
387. Transcendence
388. Trust
389. Trustworthiness
390. Truth
391. Understanding
392. Unflappability
393. Uniqueness
394. Unity
395. Usefulness
396. Utility
397. Valor
398. Variety
399. Victory
400. Vigor

401. Virtue
402. Vision
403. Vitality
404. Vivacity
405. Volunteering
406. Warm-heartedness
407. Warmth
408. Watchfulness
409. Wealth
410. Willfulness
411. Willingness
412. Winning
413. Wisdom
414. Wittiness
415. Wonder
416. Worthiness
417. Youthfulness
418. Zeal

CHAPTER FOUR
What's NOT Said Is Important Too.

Emboldened by my success with Jeanne, I tried it with Paul.

Some get lost in story. Details, more details, tangents, it's easy to get so far off track that I forget what I'm listening for. I even forget to ask questions. The story rolls on and on and I'm writing feverishly trying to capture it all.

Paul is someone who likes story. He is extremely intelligent, curious, and always mentally active. What doesn't help is that he's "on" 24/7 for work; he always has to be sharp. This makes it extremely difficult for him (or me!) to understand what's important. He's not very imaginative either.

I took a breath and began. "Sit quietly for a moment and let your thoughts go. Pay attention to your breathing and focus on it." When I could hear him steady his breath I knew he would be able to access his memories. "Tell me about a peak experience from childhood, a really fond memory, a good time, a time when you were at your best. It doesn't have to be the best memory of childhood, so no pressure. When something comes to mind tell me."

After a split second he blurted, "Well, that's not easy to do. A lot of my childhood was uneventful, the same. You know, I didn't do much just kind of got through school, got through the day . . . now you say when I was at my best, is that like winning a contest or something? I don't really know what you're asking." I attempted again to engage his senses. His mind was doing its usual intrusion, and his Saboteurs had taken over— the one that always said, "Compared to everyone else, I'm not that special." The other Saboteur voice was the one that always said, "If you're asking me to feel, then I'm going to fail."

What's a Saboteur you ask? Through the field of positive psychology, Shirzad Chamine, a Stanford professor, emerged with his work on our inner world of Saboteur and Sage with the book, *Positive Intelligence, Why Only 20% of Teams and Individuals Achieve Their True Potential and How You Can Achieve Yours.* Reading this was a life-changer for me. He explains that everyone has Saboteurs, no matter what your experience was in childhood. It's just a fact of life, call it a gift from your survivor brain. Your Saboteurs are the voices or thoughts that are meant to protect you, helped you survive emotionally and physically through childhood, but no longer serve you. They keep you small, they criticize anything you do or think that creates uncertainty. They hate uncertainty. When you take a creative risk, or step toward personal growth they are there to stop you; after all that's their job. They judge you, they judge others, they judge situations. According to the research of professor Chamine, there are ten in total. Yes, TEN. It's important to recognize Saboteurs so that we can step past them and not take them seriously especially when you're listening for values.

Controller, Hyper-Achiever, Hyper-Rational, Hyper-Vigilent, Restless, Stickler, Pleaser, Victim, Avoider, and Judge. Judge is the most important and everyone has this one plus several others as accomplices. Scary! While I could go into great detail here and how to counter the Saboteur's effect on your life, this is all you need to know for now. They will pop up later too, when you're about to experience something on your list. Please visit his site, positiveintelligence.com to learn more. Here's what you need to know for now:

The Judge, the master Saboteur

"The Judge is the universal Saboteur that afflicts everyone. It is the one that beats you up repeatedly over mistakes or shortcomings, warns you obsessively about future risks, wakes you up in the middle of the night worrying, gets you fixated on what is wrong with others or your life, etc. Your Judge is your greatest internal enemy, activates your other top Saboteurs, causes you much of your stress and unhappiness, and reduces your effectiveness."

Unless you're a trained coach or therapist, don't try to work with them. You can recognize them with a few words and phrases that serve as "red flags." Words and phrases such as "should," "could have," "have to," "must," "ought to," or anything negatively judging you, others, or life in general. Trust me, don't tangle with these buggers. Simply take your story teller back on a positive track by asking, what's important about this time? Or, tell me about . . . (whatever happened before they derailed). This is also why it's important to partner with someone who can listen to our memories. Saboteurs keep us from our creative thinking and it's impossible to be minding those ourselves while at the same time trying to envision a memory, stay open, feel joyful .

I continued. "Paul, do you know what joy feels like?"

"Well, it depends on what you mean (his mind intruding again). Do you mean like over the moon? Or just happy, like I like what I'm having for lunch?"

"Let's shoot for over the moon," I said. Several awkward seconds passed while I waited in silence.

"Okay, well, there was a day that I got to do everything I liked and that was unusual." He stopped there.

"Go on," I urged him.

"I don't know why, but I got to go swimming with my friends, then we had a picnic, then after that we went to the movies, and then to an arcade."

"What's important about that?" I asked.

"Well, not only was I doing all the things I loved, but I was there with my brother and my friends."

"Tell me more."

"I don't know what you really want to know here. It was fun."

"What is it about swimming that you like?"

"Oh, well of course I like being in the water, there's no noise, it's peaceful just me and the waves, the color is beautiful, I get a really good work out, and it just *is*."

"What do you mean by, 'it just *is*'?"

"It's the ocean, it doesn't need us, it is full of all kinds of life, it's mysterious and the sound of it is calming. You know, no one can interrupt us with texts or phone calls."

"What about the arcade was important?"

"I'm a really good aim, even back then before I had learned to shoot in the military, I could hit any target. Even those water pistols shooting at the pop-up targets. I would always bet those guys their tickets and I always walked out with the biggest prize." He smiled as he said, "the biggest prize." There was a lot of pride in his ability. Those words told me that he felt good showing everyone else that he was really good at the games.

He continued with his story about that day, and I continued being curious about what specifically made it a peak experience, something that thirty plus years later he still remembers fondly. The values I heard were NATURE, VARIETY, CONNECTION, ACHIEVEMENT, and HEALTH. When I checked those out with him, he was astonished. Especially by the value VARIETY. He became excited and engaged. I could hear it in his voice.

"Yeah, that would be amazing, if I could let's say, do nine rounds of golf, go for a swim, have a picnic with my friends at the beach, then later go to the shooting range. Now *that's* a 10 day." ACHIEVEMENT came from how proud he felt at imagining that he could achieve doing all that in one day.

I realize that you may be thinking, how's he going to do that every day? Stay with me, we're only at the beginning of this journey. At this point it's important to reach for the stars. We will narrow and edit later. What's important here is that you learn to listen, really listen, and begin to recognize values when you hear them.

Now you try it. Find a YouTube video and practice listening. Switch levels intentionally and see what you notice. Notice your thoughts first. Then their words. Then their voice, body language (no need to get lost in what body language means, just notice posture—that's enough).

When you can get the gist of it, practice this in person the next time you have a conversation with a friend, or a child (children can be easy because they're expressive and they don't self-edit). Leave practicing with your partner till a bit later. That's a little tougher because it's harder to self-manage your feelings and assumptions (Level One).

The key when listening in Levels Two and Three (even conversationally) is to keep your questions short and few, to let them know they're heard with great interest so that they feel safe to express whatever is on their mind. Their feelings about specific things gives you lots of information. When listening for values in order to create a bucket list I recommend culling from three memories: first, a memory from childhood, then young adult, then a recent memory. It's surprising how the values from childhood endure. Ideally, you'll hear five to ten and will have to see which ones stand out and which ones are expressing the same thing. You can group those. In other words, if you hear values such as art, sunsets, beautiful places, and atmosphere, you can pull all those together into the value: BEAUTY. You'll have the opportunity to be more specific in a moment.

CHAPTER FIVE
Dead On.

Two months after creating our bucket list, we had the opportunity to experience one of our big items. We went for a week to Curacao to celebrate Jan's birthday. I had had the idea to go before we created our list, but wrestled with the expense, getting the time off, should we/shouldn't we? After we created our bucket list and posted it on our bedroom wall where we could contemplate it, we realized that this trip was not just some fantasy for which we couldn't justify the cost. This was an experience that hit six of our combined values. We knew this experience would be a "10."

Or would it?

We had arrived at 11:00 pm and could not see a thing while landing, nor could we see much on our way to the hotel. It looked unremarkable. Taking a chance as we did, relying on photos and other people's opinions of the place, we were really unsure if it would be what we'd hoped: a Caribbean paradise. Oddly, as the suspense of discovering this place was building, we also realized that if we were wrong, it didn't matter. Our value of ADVENTURE was part of the experience and this certainly qualified. There would also surely be other values that would be honored that we could count on by the excursions we planned.

The taxi turned a final corner around a large curved highway after passing industrial buildings, oil refineries, tin-roof communities, and the silhouettes of cacti. Suddenly before us stood a collection of Dutch colonial, two-story homes, colorfully painted, adorned with strings of white lights. The echo of music was in the air, while potted palms swayed. A feeling of intense delight and wonder took us over. The taxi came to a stop in front of three of these gorgeous buildings. Ours was curb yellow with white accents, and the adjoining building was a vivid green. As we wheeled our bags through the star-lit walkway between them, we were greeted by an older gentleman with a wiry frame, dark skin, and white shirt, who was eager to take us in. Apparently, he'd been expecting us. The entrance to an open-air dining room was marked by bold, pink, bougainvillea flowers that adorned the top edge of a privacy screen, created from a turquoise painted fence. A conga line of beautifully dressed people shuffled by and Jan and I looked at each other grinning, ear to ear. This was definitely gonna be fun. We stood for a minute watching when a young, tall, blond, bearded gentleman with a wide smile greeted us in English. After having flown for about six hours without a scrap of food we were famished and asked him if the kitchen was still open. If not, a piece of bread would do nicely. He assured us he could find something, and instructed us to meet him here after we settled in.

Fifteen minutes later we stood like school children in a lunch line. Our host emerged from the kitchen. Eager to please, and apologetic about the wedding reception going on, he asked if we would be comfortable on a small patio facing the street, away from the wedding, as he gestured toward the setting he had created. He had set up a private table at the front of the hotel among the potted palms facing the gorgeously colorful buildings and a small winding street we hadn't seen until that moment. The manager, now our personal concierge, arrived with bowls of heavenly risotto accented with colorful beet chips. He also presented us with a large wine bucket.

"I took the liberty of choosing a Pinot Grigio that I thought would go well with this dish. Is that okay?"

"Sure" is what came out in unison. What we were thinking was, *Are you friggin' kidding? This is paradise!* To this point we hadn't even seen the restaurant, the ocean, anything of our surroundings, but we were already in love with our boutique hotel.

Morning arrived, and we could hardly stand the suspense any longer. Where were we? Was it all we had hoped? We wandered downstairs, past the housekeeper in the hallway who hunched over as she mopped the broken tiled floor original to this former home. The tiny hallway squeezed us out into the abundant warm sunlight of the patio. Gone were the bougainvillea's, gone were the candles and the beautifully dressed people in the conga line. It was peaceful. The place looked entirely different. How in the world did they accomplish this transformation without us hearing so much as a glass clink? What we saw were long weathered wooden tables, decorative glass vases with curly branches of drift wood, clean linen napkins, and large umbrella canopies shading European-looking diners. Accenting several tables were natural wood boards holding a breakfast of homemade breads, and jams. At the furthest edge, what we couldn't even hear over the music the night before, was the ocean.

We must have looked like Dorothy when she awakens to find herself in Oz. Walking to the edge of the patio we could finally see turquoise waves crashing on gigantic rocks that lined the lower patio. Crabs scurried in and around the rocks and it became clear why no one was sitting there! Truly, this place was paradise.

The rest of our trip unfolded with the same anticipation and adventure of a completely new place. What did "just down the road" mean? How many beaches were there, and were they swimmable? Is the local language Dutch or Spanish or some combination? Oh, it's

Papiamento. Is that Venezuela we see? Where should we not walk at night? The entire week we fantasized about returning with the kids (another value) or buying a place. Could we start a permaculture farm? (Another value.) Each day a "10," right up to the moment we boarded the plane home.

This experience alone proved the value of the bucket list. Realizing that this list also served as a way to evaluate opportunities of all kinds made it a very practical tool. Now we had the means to know how much money, time or effort would the experience be worth. No regrets. As our trip began to unfold in Curacao, we knew we were dead on with our assessment of what would be a fulfilling experience.

However, your homecoming may feel a little different after one of your "10" experiences.

Arriving in Miami the fantasy ended. Border guards in a surprise random check stood positioned across the wide hall. This was AFTER we had already cleared Border Control and Customs. Our re-entry into the U.S. struck a chord of fear in us, U.S. citizens. We could imagine the terror of any foreigner facing this intended intimidation. The surge of adrenaline became a sharp contrast to the peaceful, harmonious dream we had been living. Then the TV ads at every gate blared. The non-stop bombardment of advertising ran unceasing through the background of every area we entered. This mind-numbing brainwash to buy, buy, buy! reminded us we had returned.

The taxi ride home from the airport in Philly wasn't any better. At 1:00 a.m. fourteen inches from my face, a TV screen ran ad after ad, blinding me. I felt around for a button or a touch screen "off" switch and realized I had no way to turn off the glaring light and noise. What happened to my freedom of choice? Oh boy, re-entry.

I recognize it from the days we returned home from Brazil where my husband, children and I lived for two years. Sharp criticism of your own culture intrudes no matter where you return from. It takes time to adjust again, close your mind and ears to the stinging clarity you have when confronted by your culture as though for the first time. You may begin to long for a place that is foreign, a place you initially feared and felt uncertain, a place you had to open your mind to discover. Well, guess what? You now have to muster that same wonder and curiosity coming home.

Re-entry shock. We never anticipated that.

Just know that as you begin to live some of your big bucket list experiences, life will look different when you return to the normal day to day. It's not predictable how, or what will look different either. You will have lived an experience that is truly peak which means that ordinary life, as good as it is, will pale by comparison. Don't let it fool you. *Remember that this is a temporary culture shock that will pass.* You will love your home, your ordinary life again, I promise, especially if you have managed to incorporate your bucket list into every day as I will show you how to do shortly. Your life will go from okay, to good, to great, to extraordinary in a short time. The big items, the fantasy items, when you attain them—and trust me, it will happen sooner than you ever imagined—have a re-entry factor.

Life slowly returned to normal, but we were forever changed. We felt initially gutted and fantasized about returning to Curacao. This sort of thing with a little distance and perspective looks like running away to me. Remember when I mentioned dissociating? Jan and I were dissociating by fantasizing about how we could live in Curacao, maybe retire there. If that idea is going to be a sound idea and not a regret, it will still be a good idea if you sit with it for a few years. Try it out in a smaller way. Perhaps rent a house for a month and see how that feels before pulling up stakes and altering your life completely.

We will definitely return to Curacao, and would love to bring our kids with us. The place has so many beautiful qualities that resonate with us. To lift ourselves back to loving life day to day, we returned once again to our bucket list and looked at some of the smaller items, things that we could do in an evening or on a weekend. What we discovered is that there really is an art to dreaming small. Paradoxically, the first step is dreaming big. We'll talk about this more in Chapter Nine.

Hang on, and keep reaching for the stars. Are you ready?

CHAPTER SIX
Narrow, Expand, Then Narrow Again.

Narrowing

So now that you have your list of five to ten values, list them in priority. How you do that is to put them in a first-draft order, then start at the top and work your way down. Look at your first and second values and ask yourself, would I give up "this" (second value) for "this" (first value)? If the answer is no, then your second value becomes your first. Work your way down the list and don't worry if it's exactly right.

Choose your top five. Then ask yourself if any of the others can be rolled into your top five. In other words, are they expressing the same thing? For example, I had FAMILY, PARTNER, and FRIENDSHIP on my list and I found it impossible to choose between them. Finally, I combined them into a value I call CONNECTION because intimate connection was at the heart of all three values.

By contrast, I also had BEAUTY and NATURE. I thought about it because where I find the most extraordinary beauty is in nature. It took a lot of thinking about what I find beautiful and what I meant specifically. It turns out that I also meant things like art, design, architecture, music, fashion, photography, and theatre. Nature remained in its own category, so I kept both.

While it may be tempting to want to keep them all, what you will end up with is so expansive (because you'll be expanding again), I don't want you to be overwhelmed. You can always do another bucket list once you've experienced everything on your first list. Or reinvigorate your list by adding in another value, or replacing one. A list of five values takes several hours. These can be exhausting hours, but fun though. It took us several days over about a month to create ours. Of course, as I was developing this we hit some dead-ends and had to go back and retry. Hopefully, because of our dead-ends yours will go a whole lot faster.

Expand

What we're going to do now is a brainstorming exercise. Take your list of five values (or if you have less time you can choose only three) and write at the top of a large sheet of paper (two per sheet so you wind up with three large sheets) that you can post to the wall. (PostIt pads 33" x 36" are expensive so you can use a large pad of craft paper and tape it).

My gut tells me, yet, to date I haven't found the research to validate this, that the size of your paper is very important because it requires movement to write. What I have found about it is in the field of science called Embodied Cognition. It's a new theory, developed in the 1990's and it is still evolving.

Here is what I found in *Scientific American*, "A Brief Guide to Embodied Cognition: Why You Are Not Your Brain" by Samuel McNerney on November 4, 2011.

"Term Assistant Professor of Psychology Joshua Paul, who teaches at Barnard College and focuses on embodiment [was asked,] what the future of embodiment studies looks like . . . 'whereas sensory inputs and motor outputs were secondary, we now see them as integral to cognitive processes.'

Dr. Gail Matthews, a psychology professor at the Dominican University in California, found that you become "42% more likely to achieve your goals and dreams by writing them down on a regular basis."

Dr. Gail Matthews did a study of 267 people, both men and women, from all over the world and divided them into two groups: those who wrote down their goals and dreams and those who didn't. The results were astounding. Those who wrote down their goals were 42% more likely to achieve them. Paraphrased here in an article in the *Huffington Post* is the explanation of why that is:

"This is significant, because if you just THINK about one of your goals or dreams, you're only using the right hemisphere of your brain, which is your imaginative center. But, if you . . . write it down, you also tap into the power of your logic-based left hemisphere and you send your consciousness . . . a signal that says, 'I want this, and I mean it!'"
— Mary Morrissey, *Huffington Post*

My hypothesis is that writing on a large piece of paper on the wall requires movement: using your body, using open strokes, arm raised, room to move by walking away and looking, is a combination of what Dr. Gail Matthews found, and Assistant Professor of Psychology Joshua Paul's theory of Embodied Cognition. I can't help but think that if movement helps you to grasp abstract concepts and writing them down increases your likelihood of achieving your goals and dreams, then the combination must be even more effective.

Before you start, you need a partner to scribe and participate in brainstorming. Let's face it, you can't "brainstorm" by yourself or you'd end up with light sprinkle. Your partner can be your intimate partner, as I had mentioned earlier, if you have an open, accepting, non-judgmental relationship. If you tend to criticize one another you're better off working with a friend or bucket list buddy. Your brainstorming partner will stand at the posted paper on the wall, color marker in hand (you may want to use a different color for each value list because later you can use colors to check off similar or repeat ideas that appear in different value expressions lists). Your partner will then set a timer for 3 minutes. The urgency helps to stimulate thinking because throwing out ideas takes risk and if you know the clock is ticking you're more likely to throw something— *anything*—out there.

That's the idea. Better to be absurd and fill that sheet than be careful to make these ideas "great" and have only a few to choose from. Your brainstorming partner will also contribute ideas to keep things moving and to stimulate your thinking. When an idea is thrown out, the response should be positive and building on the last idea such as, "Yes!" or, "Good!" or, "Yes, and . . . " You will ultimately choose from this list so you can discard any of them later. You'll be surprised at what comes up under these circumstances.

Have FUN. After all, this is your bucket list! If you're having difficulty getting started, tell each other an embarrassing story. This technique has been proven to enhance creativity. It's all about feeling safe to take a risk. It's explained here in this excerpt from an article in smartcompany.com:

"Research outlined by Kellogg School of Management at Northwestern University professor Leigh Thompson in the *Harvard Business Review* explores how people can be primed for better brainstorming and points to the effectiveness of candour in generating greater creativity.

Thompson and colleagues Elizabeth Ruth Wilson and Brian Lucas conducted a number of experiments in which participants were required to share personal experiences before tackling a brainstorming session.

Thompson writes that the researchers hypothesized that 'the "embarrassing story" condition would lead people to drop their inhibitions and get more creative.'

Output was measured in terms of idea fluency and flexibility, and the embarrassing stories group led the way, scoring 7.4 for fluency and 5.5 for flexibility, compared those in the group that had discussed pride, which scored 5.843 and 4.568.

'We suspected that the effects might be magnified if the recounting of accomplishments caused people to worry more about hierarchy and social comparisons, quelling creativity, and if a discussion of foibles helped people to open up and take more risks, boosting brainstorming efficacy,' Thompson explains."[6]

---

[6] Want your team to brainstorm better? Share your most embarrassing moment first, by Martin Kovacs, Wednesday, October 4, 2017

If your bucket list partner is already a good friend or your intimate partner, I'm sure they already know your embarrassing stories, so dive right in.

Overarching Values

Have a look at your entire list and find the values that must be included in *every* value to make it true for you. This is often an assumption because it is a built-in, automatic perspective for you which is why it is so important to identify. Especially if you plan to experience your bucket list with a partner or friend. They may think you mean one thing, and you're assuming another.

For example, we looked at our values of ADVENTURE, NATURE, BEAUTY, IDEA REALIZATION, CELEBRATION, and CONNECTION. What we realized after brainstorming the expression of each is that what was true for every one of them is AUTHENTICITY. For us, and I emphasize that these are our values—someone else may love the expressions that I'm going to describe here and I have no judgement about it—if any of these expressions were taking place in artificial or manmade environments such as in taking a cruise, visiting zoos or game parks, themed chain restaurants, or somehow in shopping centers that are created to look like a town center (and are often named Town Center), we would not be happy with the experience. To us, AUTHENTICITY had to be built into each expression. In fact, AUTHENTICITY was our assumption with everything. We just hadn't realized it until I challenged our list. Glad we happened to be thinking the same way.

Once you've brainstormed the expressions of your values and you have three to five columns of multiple and varied ways that those values are epitomized, you can now narrow your list. What you're looking for is no more than three expressions of each value. You can usually combine a few and give it one name. For example, in our values expression lists for NATURE, ADVENTURE and BEAUTY we had written "blue water" twice, "warm water," and "exotic location." This became "blue water" meaning Caribbean blue water which is both warm and exotic.

If you ever decide to add to your bucket list or create a new one, you can always return to these lists. It's amazing how much you can squeeze out of this list as it has come from your values and it stimulates all kinds of cool ideas. We had to return to it a couple of times when we actually forgot what we meant by the item we wrote on our final bucket list.

So, save it or photograph it for future reference.

CHAPTER SEVEN
Best Of

Now that you've got this crazy list, it's time to choose what is truly meaningful and exciting.

When Jeanne and I brainstormed her list we made two mistakes. Being that this was a relatively new method still in experimentation, I tried allowing for more time in brainstorming. That was mistake number one. Jeanne is a very thoughtful, contemplative person. She likes to first think of something, then check in with her body to notice how it feels. Jeanne would then search for a more accurate word to express her thought. This took time. It also took the fun and energy out of brainstorming too. It felt arduous and took us several hours over two sessions. *Brainstorming is not a perfecting process.* It's a messy, fast, fun, open, creative, playful process where anything goes. The best ideas always arise out of something you gave little thought to, otherwise you wouldn't need to brainstorm. It fetches ideas from the far reaches of your mind, from a place where you wouldn't logically look. Timing forces action which is a key component. There's excitement, a little anxiety ("Hey, don't rush me! This is going to be the most important experiences of my life!"). It's counter intuitive, but trust me it works. Rush.

Our second mistake was including adjectives. Words like "safe" and "extraordinary" were bucket list *killers*. When we narrowed Jeanne's list, I couldn't quite name why those items should not be selected. It eventually became clear when we tried to imagine what doing "safe" meant. Yeah, nothing. We eventually selected the nouns and verbs and created a doable, enjoyable List.

Remember: no adjectives; no more than three minutes.

Your expressions list may be long: there's a lot that you can brainstorm in three minutes. You may have gotten stuck and only produced a handful of items. It actually doesn't matter. This selection process can work even if your brainstorming only resulted in a handful of items. Very likely you've come up with several variations on one theme.

For example, this was our (mine and Jan's) brainstormed list under the value IDEA REALIZATION:

> Legos, building, rehabbing, business, invention, travel, charity, art, garbage, oceans, build-a-?, children, book, workshop, family get-together, X-mas, teaching, healing, water, conservation, animals, civic participation, womens' self-reliance.

Yes, somehow, we brainstormed children, oceans, water, and travel in this category too. Not only did these not seem to have anything to do with IDEA REALIZATION (at the time it did!), but we also had three of these items (oceans, water, and travel) appear under ADVENTURE, BEAUTY and NATURE. When we got to choosing a best-of, we didn't select them, however, these items became more important to pay attention to when we got to those other values that also produced them. We wanted to make sure they made it into a top three selection of another category so we used check marks, color coded, to represent its value to see how important it was and where else it appeared.

What you're trying to do is avoid repetition in your final selection. Save these lists. You may go back to them not only to figure out what you meant for an item that makes it onto your bucket list, but to add to or expand your list once you've ticked off a number of items.

Trust me, ticking off experiences happens faster than you think.

The other narrowing activity is to combine items that are alike. For example, we had "blue water" "warm" and "beaches" under NATURE. We combined these into "blue water" which became one of our top three. Another example is "building." Under IDEA REALIZATION we had brainstormed "building," "rehabbing," "build-a-?," and "civic participation." That became "build." Then in the same value category, "oceans," "garbage," "charity," "conservation," and "civic participation" were combined into "conservation" after we discussed what we had in mind when we threw out each idea. The core of those words was really "conservation" in some form. That's the only thing that would motivate us to look at garbage!

"Art" also appeared in IDEA REALIZATION, and surely because I am an artist, that is my mindset for almost anything I do. That's not to say that creating art, painting specifically, needs to be part of everything I do to make it meaningful. For me it means looking at the world through an artistic lens. Creativity is almost impossible for me to separate and do only in a studio. It's the juice in everything I do. "Art" also appears in our BEAUTY category. It ended up being so much a part of my thinking, and a big value of Jan's, yet it didn't actually make our top three in IDEA REALIZATION, but appeared in several forms on our final bucket list.

All this is to tell you, don't worry. What's important will, one way or another, make it to your final list. Remember, this is your list. No one will ever care what's on your list except maybe your partner and there's a way to combine your bucket lists. In fact, I highly recommend it. (I go into that a bit more in the last chapter if you want to skip ahead.)

At the end of this part of the exercise, things were starting to take shape and look exciting. Ironically, this is where Jan and I got stuck! What we're about to do in the next two chapters is the magic to this method if there is one magical step. It's also why "dreaming small" will make sense. For now, scan your best-of choices, circle them in another color and make sure you have variety. We had check marks on some of the items on our list. Our heads were swimming with which category we wanted to have the items appear that we had written in several places, and really how important something was. So, for example, "invention" had four checks, "build-a-?" had three. We looked at our circled items (because we had too many) and tried to see if an item could also reflect another VALUE category. Using the check marks to tell us how important the item was helped. Again, remember that you'll save these lists to refer to after you've created your bucket list, to understand what you meant or to build more into the areas you've already experienced.

This is a "living" bucket list. It's meant to guide you, excite you, inform you, and help you acknowledge all the great things you've done and those you'll do. It's not static, and it is *not meant to be done at the end of your life!*

To borrow a cliche, "There's no time like the present" so live now.

CHAPTER EIGHT
Person, Place, or Thing?

Working with Paul on this was very different.

Paul and I started very slowly with a couple of failed attempts. He needs to examine the process and understand exactly what we're aiming for before he can free his mind. This may be your experience too. It's okay! He was happy with concentrating on only three values categories, however his prolific mind brainstormed twenty-six items for MUSIC alone, each usable. Here's a small sample:

> "concerts, open-air, trumpet, jazz, lessons, dance!, drums, jam, radio, composing, singing, opera, Broadway..."

Then for NATURE we brainstormed about as many. Here's another sampling:

> "estuaries, land, water on + under, science of water, fish, sea turtles, rivers, lakes, ponds, Mississippi-muddy, stormy water ..."

By the time we got to PHYSICAL ACTIVITY we were on a roll. Paul's excitement was a sharp contrast to his normally monotone voice when talking about his day-to-day routine. What had become clear, and a total surprise when we initially explored his values, was that VARIETY was the one factor than amplified each experience. Therefore, it became his umbrella or overarching value. While Paul wanted to keep almost all of what he brainstormed, (and remember to keep your list so you can return to it to continue creating) it became much more effective to have him choose his most exciting ideas, and the idea that truly represented each value. We circled about five for each because he was working with only three values. In Paul's abbreviated bucket-list creation we played with combining several things, in different order. For him, there was no need to go much further. He wanted to try some of these ideas first. He got so excited at what we were brainstorming that he wanted to pause our work and dive into the experiences. This was like breathing life back into his tired soul. To see him eager to plan the weekend or an evening with his girlfriend, like a gathering at the beach, is what made all my effort worthwhile. While you may be tempted to pause here like he did, I would say that you have nothing to lose by following through with this entire method to see what you can create. Momentum and collaboration with your bucket list partner is something that can fizzle. As Arnold Schwartzenegger in *Predator* would say, "Do it. Do it NOW."

What you'll do to continue creating your bucket list, is to group these value expressions that you just brainstormed. I'll explain: once you've chosen three epitome expressions of each value (or five if you're working with fewer values) is to group them into noun and verb categories labeled "People, Place, Thing and Activity." When Jan and I created our list, we changed People to Beings so that we could include animals and spirit. You may want to keep yours as People.

The reason for grouping, is so that you end up with building blocks that you can combine. Realize, you're organizing a massive amount of information in ways that you can play with it, move it around, combine it, but simplify it.

Our groupings numbered six because we had two "Place" groupings and two "Activity" groupings after we decided to group them in threes. At the time, we created smaller groups to make more even blocks on the matrix (which, by the way, is where they will end up) not knowing it would actually be a good idea. Break your groups into three expressions each. You can have multiple groups of People, Place, Thing or Activity. Another thing we did is to combine Family and Friends as one expression as Family/Friends. That's because there are some family members who we enjoy so much that they feel like friends, and some friends we are so close to that they feel like family. To narrow who we intend to share experiences with, we combined them.

Anyway, here were our Being, Place, Thing, and Activity groupings:

> Being: Animal, Family/Friends, Spirit
>
> Place: 1) Amazon Tree House, Ice Hotel, Blue
> Water
> 2) Redwoods, Caves, Exotic Location
>
> Thing: Music, Flowers, Candles
>
> Activity: 1) Build, Invention, Conservation
> 2) Party, Recognition, Dedication

Now you're ready to put them on a matrix. Across the very top, above the actual matrix to make sure your values never get lost in the particulars, write each value. Then if there are any overarching values (no more than two) write those below them, centered. When it comes time to make decisions about what you'll invest time, effort or money in you want to make sure that these are present. Down the left side, list your Person, Place, Thing and Activity groupings. You can do it in any order, in fact, on our bucket list we listed ours randomly. It doesn't matter. When each expression grouping is listed, draw a line below it all the way across your matrix. This is why it's helpful to have only three-per group. These will become your building blocks.

Now you're ready to move across the top.

CHAPTER NINE
The Art of Dreaming Small

This is tried and true. At first, we listed our values across the top of the matrix columns with them repeated down the side. It made sense. Then when we started to create combinations of values with expressions of values, what was created was redundancy. After that first dead-end, we listed the expressions across the top. Talk about mind-blowing minutia! We knew this step would be critical.

Have you ever read *Blue Ocean Strategy* written by W. Chan Kim and Renee Mauborgne? It's a great example of using a matrix for innovation. When companies are stuck and need to open up thinking around creating products or services that are so unique that they no longer have competitors, this is a brilliant exercise. The magic happens because of what you pair (across the top, and down the side when each meets). This was my inspiration.

Getting it right was well worth hitting a few dead-ends. After all, we are innovating a way to live your life to its fullest and most meaningful expression. Thinking about coaching and building momentum toward a goal, creating a new habit, or taking measured risks, it occurred to me that sampling your list by starting small and building from there makes sense. It's practical because putting a huge amount of time, effort and money toward a new experience seems risky. The more time, effort, and money it takes, the more likely it is that you'll be waiting a long time before you actually do it. Living for someday is unhealthy. The most important moment you have is now.

This is where this method and the traditional bucket list part ways.

Remember what my thinking was when my clients first came to me with this request? The only reference I had for why you would want to create a bucket list was that you were facing a terminal illness. Compelled by imminent doom to finally live, you would create a list of experiences that represent what you might regret not experiencing.

This bucket list is only the beginning. It's a way to start living creatively and enjoyably according to what's most important, then continue designing your life.

Back to creating your list, across the top of the columns in order to create sections, write "Small" "Medium" and "Large." Then if you want to add "Dreams" go right ahead. We decided not to because living our largest expressions felt like living "the dream."

Next is another bit of brainstorming. Begin with your first epitome expression and ask yourself, "How can I do this today, tomorrow, or this weekend?" to fill the first column, the Small category. For example, our first epitome expression was "Amazon Tree House." Now you may ask, and we certainly did, *how in the hell can you do Amazon Tree House today, tomorrow, or this weekend?* This is where having your values across the top comes in. We asked ourselves where that expression came from and realized that the whole point of Amazon Tree House would be to experience nature, and not just any nature, but something extraordinary. After pondering for a moment, sleeping under the stars could be done certainly by the weekend in the warmer months ahead. Our usual camping spots would need to be revisited for the "extraordinary" part. Maybe it could be in an environment that was a little more remote than our usual spots. Maybe in could be more "hotel" like by bringing our down pillows and tray table for a night stand? If we really wanted a hotel experience we could invest in a larger tent, and shocker: "glamp." We smiled and realized that this would be just perfect.

We used to laugh at "glampers," thinking, why bother camping? What we were learning about ourselves was that AUTHENTICITY meant that a camping trailer with a full kitchen, shower, bed, etc.... was telling us that the convenience aspect felt like it was removing us from nature, i.e., sleeping under the stars. Funny, it never occurred to us before that you could "glamp" in other ways that allowed you to enjoy some comforts and gourmet treats while experiencing nature. Bingo.

Continuing across our matrix to the "Medium" box, we thought about experiencing the "Amazon Tree House" a little farther from home, perhaps in another state. There were places all across the country we had never been: national parks in the west, or near where we live. Come to think of it, there's a national park where wild ponies wander freely on a beach where you can camp: Assateague Island in Maryland (that crosses into Virginia). Our thinking had opened up. The idea of a hotel however, kept nagging at us. Time to Google "tree house hotels." Lo and behold there are actually tree house hotels in Texas and South Carolina that take an under-the-stars nature experience to a whole new level. Not cheap though. So now we have several possibilities to explore. We kept this idea in the back of our minds knowing it may make sense in another category. Satisfied with camping (in our new comfort style with a bigger tent and more comfortable accessories) at Chincoteague National Wild Refuge in Virginia, on the beach and seeing the wild ponies would be a "10." Now, the "Large" category was easy: stay in the Amazon Tree House hotel in Brazil. It's not a dream because we know we can do it, but it's going to take all kinds of resources to make it happen. Perfect.

Next expression on our list was much more difficult: The Ice Hotel in Iceland. Using our imagination, we stood and contemplated what exactly that experience meant. A friend of mine stayed there and told me about it which was the first time I'd ever heard of it. As she spoke I pictured cavernous spaces aglow like when Superman brings Louis Lane to his lair. Extraordinary, and only possible close to the Arctic. Then my friend described fur bed covers, fur rugs, hot springs, iced vodka drinks— I had never heard of anything so luxurious or exotic. Yes, that would be an epitome experience worthy of the "Large" category, but how do you do "Ice Hotel" in "Small?" Our wheels were turning which helped us spit out all kinds of cold, snowy, cozy place ideas. I'm no skier, or much of a skater, so I started getting Christmassy scenes in my mind, cold, cozy, merry and bright.

"I got it. How about a cabin somewhere upstate New York or Vermont?"

Jan responded, "New York is closer and if we're going for 'Small' then let's stay even closer like the Poconos." We were onto something.

"Okay, so we rent a cabin in December or January, buy a couple of those fake fur rugs from IKEA, bring that crystal bar set we never use that you inherited from your dad, candles . . . maybe go with some friends?" My voice high-pitched with excitement I squealed, "Bring Icelandic vodka, and create an Icelandic-themed menu!"

The more we brainstormed the more fun we realized we could have. That's the idea. While what we were brainstorming wasn't without cost, comparatively to the original idea, it was immediately doable for us and a fun trip unto itself. Creating this list gave us permission to be creative and imaginative, even indulgent. Why not? I remember the ideas and fun I put into my kids' birthday parties, finding a way to make my own decorations, games and party favors. Now that they're grown I seem to be in a rut. We have dinner parties and enjoy entertaining friends, but I have been feeling like I've been uninspired in planning our get togethers. Entertaining can be costly. I don't mind saving for something that I'm looking forward to because half the fun (for me) is in the planning. This kind of gathering would be worth it.

Now for the "Medium" category. Hmmm. We had to really think of what is cool (no pun intended) about being in a hotel made of ice. "The atmosphere is more important than the cold for me; having a view of nature, actually more like wilderness, while being protected and comfortable . . . "

Jan picked up on my thought, ". . . being in a bubble of sorts, a fish bowl, with a view of nature. How about that train in Canada?"

"What?!" I'd never heard of a train in Canada that might even come close to this kind of experience, which piqued my interest.

"Yeah," he continued. "My dad did it and we have home movies of it. There's a large bubble that you can sit in like a lounge, and you cross all kinds of wilderness."

That was it! That sounded extraordinary, and we could fly inexpensively or drive to Toronto. I don't know how much the train costs, but it would be worth looking into. I say this realizing that categorizing this experience as "Medium" may be someone else's "Large" because of distance or expense. It's all relative. Perhaps the cabin idea is more of a "Medium" to you, and you would be challenged to think of a "Small" version. That's where brainstorming with someone makes it so much fun. You have to get pretty creative with some of these small and medium categories. It's easy to think extravagantly, but to really make this work for you you'll need to create a day, evening, or weekend version, whatever that means to you. For example, if travel to a snowy wilderness is out of the question, try an IMAX movie or turning your dining room into a crystal palace and having someone over to dinner. The idea that you're trying out a bucket list idea would be very intriguing, and your friend (or date) would be very interested in hearing about it and why having a themed dinner that represents a larger bucket list item would be a bucket list item for you.

Whatever you do, don't let negative thinking stop you. Yes, there are obstacles like money and time, but working around those pushes your creativity. Continue across for each expression and if you get stuck, leave it blank. Keep your momentum going. Better to come back to it than to simply fill it in for the sake of completing it. What I've discovered is that having some blanks is fun especially after you've already done some of the smaller things. Your ideas may change or you may want to tweak something after an experience. You're learning more about yourself with every experience. Ideas take time to percolate too. Your subconscious will be working to fill in that blank. You'll be driving, or watching TV and all of a sudden, an idea will pop into your mind that you never would have thought. Keep your thinking about this open and fun. If you're not having fun, put it away for a while.

Your matrix should be fairly full by the end of this exercise, but you're not done yet. The real fun is about to begin!

CHAPTER TEN
Building Blocks

Paul never made it to the matrix.

It's all good though—he made it far enough that we did the same thing without formalizing each step. What he taught me was that you can do a "hack" of this and it still works. Here's how it went:

Much to Paul's amazement, when he imagined each expression of the other two value categories, MUSIC and NATURE, and paired it with a PHYSICAL ACTIVITY the experience suddenly became a "10." Then when we combined several PHYSICAL ACTIVITIES in one day, his excitement went off the charts.

We started to stack PHYSICAL ACTIVITIES and added an expression from both NATURE and MUSIC. Paul now had an endless source of ideas for bucket list-worthy experiences. The only thing he was missing as an official category was CONNECTION. A human connection. Digging deeper on this, I asked, "Is it important that you do all of this alone?" While he's a guy who enjoys solitude, he imagined having each experience alone and realized that he had been assuming that friends and family would be part of it, or at least between and at the end of these experiences.

A guy who likes the feeling of achievement, Paul imagined jamming in as many of his bucket list experiences into one day as is humanly possible. "Hmm, let's see, if I could go for a bike ride in the morning, have lunch with a friend while listening to music, go to a movie, then make dinner with my girlfriend— THAT would be my perfect day!" All of those experiences were everyday-type of experiences, something that might appear in your Small category. Combining them gave Paul VARIETY and stacking as many as possible into one day gave him the feeling of ACHEIVEMENT.

Can you see how we're using each experience in the Small, Medium, and Large categories now to build a bucket list-worthy itinerary for a day, weekend, or major event? It's not difficult now that you realize what you value most and what these values look like *in your world*. Each individual item alone is great, however, if you could experience several values in one event, the event becomes spectacular.

Your bucket list matrix will serve you well in making decisions too. Remember that trip to a wedding in Greece I told you about? Here is how we decided to go:

While I was touched to have been invited, I realized that it would require significant resources. Flights alone were in the thousands of dollars. The time difference made it so that we would have to be there for at least a week. Trying to figure out if we should go, we thought about it and discussed it quite a bit. Whenever we have a big decision to make, we refer back to our bucket list matrix and to the values across the top. Besides having written Mediterranean in our Large column, we realized that an occasion like this would honor these of our common values: CONNECTION, CELEBRATION, NATURE, BEAUTY, ADVENTURE, and the overarching value, AUTHENTICITY. That's six of our highest values. I wanted to be there for my new friend, and it also had to make sense in a bigger way. The number of combined values we would experience, plus what it would mean to my friend and our relationship, told us that it was worth the resources and effort.

After several flight searches that offered little hope of being able to pay for this, we got creative. Having family and friends in Amsterdam, we searched flights to there and found a great deal. Then flying from Amsterdam to Athens was much less expensive. It also gave us the opportunity to visit them. Deciding how long to go and arranging our schedules wasn't as difficult as we had thought being that the wedding was still six months away. Somehow, it all fell into place.

Had we not identified our values we would have thought it was a lovely gesture and would have passed up the opportunity to be there for my friend and to have an extraordinary experience. Turning her down would be the *reasonable* thing to do, right? Some people thought we were crazy. I mean, who flies across the world to see a friend they have never actually met? It was puzzling even to the groom. Evie (my friend) and I got it. Jan took a video of us seeing each other for the first time. Posting that to our small group chat, our colleagues got it. Their reaction confirmed that this wild experience was grounded in deep meaning. In England, Aruba, Toronto, New York, Spain and California, they were all touched, some in tears.

Be prepared for advice from well-meaning friends who will think you're nuts. Remember the movie *Bucket List*? Morgan Freeman's wife thinks he's nuts. She gets angry that he could be doing something so foolish when he has so little time left to live. He even questions his own desire to join Jack Nicholson because, *this is not what reasonable people do.* That's probably the kind of reaction you can expect. Most people dismiss opportunities all the time because it may seem too much trouble, too expensive, selfish maybe. They are judging you by *their* values and fears. Their Saboteur voices keep their lives within the lines of certainty, comfortable, and dull. Sometimes they're wishing that they were the ones having these incredible experiences.

And if you approach your bucket list creation like Paul did, you can increase the meaning and joy in everyday life. It's unfortunate, but some will listen to the Saboteur that says, "I'm not creative," or "this is too much work," or it's "silly." They're also the ones who will wait to do these things until it's convenient. Sadly, for most people, that day never comes.

Back to building blocks.

The reason I had you arrange each expression into People/Beings, Places, Things, and Activities is to make it easier for you to try different combinations in order to create one fabulous experience. Look across your matrix. Take a block from your Beings category in Small let's say, and imagine what it would be like to combine it with a Places block from the Medium category. Now add an Activities block. What do you get?

Jan and I did this recently when we had a weekend with nothing planned. We went to the Italian Market (it's an open-air market in Philly), and had a great time exploring Italian delicacies for a picnic. Truffle sheep's milk cheese, lemon vinaigrette, salami, New Jersey end-of-summer tomatoes, and truffle potato chips created an extraordinary menu. There was a bottle of Cotes du Rhone sitting in our cupboard left over from entertaining last fall. We brought our music outside onto our tiny balcony, spread the picnic delicacies out on our balcony table, and watched the sunset. Dinner lasted about an hour, but the pleasure of planning our menu and going to the Italian market to hunt and gather created a really fun Saturday. Of course, in Philadelphia there's always something going on especially in early fall, so being that we had already "prepared" dinner and had time in the afternoon, we strolled the art show in Rittenhouse Square (a few blocks away). The sun shining, cool air, art, gardens, then a picnic . . . it cost us less than going to a restaurant and it was perfect. See what I mean? NATURE, BEAUTY, CONNECTION,

AUTHENTICITY (in the Italian food and in the art show we strolled, the park gardens)—it was all there. To make it even better, we were remembering a beautiful picnic we had just had overlooking the Rhone in Provence from the trip we had taken to Greece (we worked our way back to Amsterdam and spent a few days in the south of France). If we wanted to go even farther with stirring that memory (instead of making an Italian picnic) we could have conjured some of the qualities with lavender (common in the south of France) and choice of music.

Now you try it. When you find a few things in the Small category, combine them, or combine one or two of them with a Medium category, and you'll see that you have something truly wonderful to look forward to, to plan, to imagine, to experience. There's an art to this imagining, combining, and reducing your Large experiences to something spectacularly Small. There's also a daring leap to be taken, to move outside your norm, to be creative and live. I commend you for getting this far. Keep it going, and tell those Saboteur to take a hike.

CHAPTER ELEVEN
Drill Down
Take It With You (Work, Couples, Etc.)

"I just want to figure out my next step" my new client laments. He is at least the fifth in the last few months to come to me not knowing which way to turn. There's always a situation to unravel, but the majority of my clients are coming to me because they've lost their internal compass. They want to work with passion, with meaning, with pride and mission.

To many of us work is important for practical reasons. For some of us it's paramount to our sense of purpose. Why can't it be both? We certainly spend a significant amount of time at it. When I am stretching my abilities, my mind won't let the challenge go and I even bring it to bed with me (I know this is not healthy, but I turn over every detail, *ad nauseum,* until I am sure I will get it right).

What if we created a bucket list matrix for our work? What if we decided what is most important about our work by naming our values? What if we named our desired destination and experiences along the way, then set out to attain those experiences?

Again, it comes down to dreaming small. I believe we have been brainwashed into thinking that everything we do has to be larger than life to have significance. When you think about it, most of our more meaningful work experiences come down to serving someone, working alongside someone, leading a handful of people. It's where we are now, right in front of us. Yet, it's the forest for the trees.

How different would we feel setting our sights on experiences we want to have based on what we value, rather than solely evaluating our efforts by how much we will earn, what skills we have, or what title we want? And if we did aim at a title or a financial figure, it would be worth digging deeper on what the title or money means and what it brings.

For me, I began to accomplish what I named on my bucket list when I focused on the values I wanted to express. Among the expressions we brainstormed, both Jan and I found several dream ideas that we didn't realize we were holding. Seeing it on paper, after a flurry of spitting out anything that comes to mind, is a revelation. It's like, "I had no idea that was in there!" Then we went back to the Small column and named smaller versions of the big ideas we had. That's truly the magic. We could then move forward to do what we needed to do in order to have those experiences. See, this is where you may be thinking that figuring out the steps to the big idea is how to get there. What we've discovered is that the smaller, related items have to stand on their own; feel complete when accomplished. No matter what happens after that, there's no way you can tell yourself, "Yeah, but I never got there." It is worthy unto itself.

Tinkering with this idea, it may be helpful to have a work-specific bucket list.

In my values category of IDEA REALIZATION, many work-related items appear as expressions of this value, such as "write a book," "workshops" and "build a tiny, self-sufficient village." While these things are happening, it makes me wonder what more I could experience if I expanded that category, then drilled down.

Inspired by the success of realizing so many extraordinary experiences, Jan and I decided to tempt fate and put some financial figures on our list. In the category of IDEA REALIZATION we had named a few work experiences we would like to accomplish. For example, I wrote, "workshop" thinking that I would like to challenge myself to give a workshop to continue to attract coaching clients, but also to be paid for it. This may not sound like a big deal to you, but for me it was. I had never given a workshop before. I had facilitated meetings and retreats for companies, but that's different. I would need to call upon those experiences to deliver an idea that could translate to something immediately valuable to individuals on a personal level. At least I could see a way to do it, so "workshop" accompanied by a dollar figure stood up to the "Risk, Requirement, Realistic" test.

Oh yeah, one last "to do" before your bucket list in finished. This is what differentiates dreams from something you can actually plan to experience. It's what I call the "Risk, Requirement, Realistic" sanity check and here's where it comes in:

Looking at our full bucket list matrix I began to wonder if I was just throwing out numbers to throw darts at or if these stretch figures could possibly be attained. On the upper right corner of our bucket list matrix I wrote "Risk, Reward, Realistic." That was my final "ah ha." As a coach I felt it was super important to know the difference between when I was fantasizing and when I was stretching my desires; I wanted to realize each experience without setting unattainable expectations or risking too much. You would think that "realistic" as a barometer would keep you too confined or uncreative. Instead, it provides a valuable sanity check and separates the fantasies from attainable dreams; it puts me and you in charge and responsible for the outcome of our named experiences, and on the flip side also credited for the outcome rather than outside forces, (i.e., God, the stars, the Universe, the powers of visualization for manifestation, or any other person or thing).

Nothing against fantasy dreams, just know the difference.

But why was putting a dollar figure on my list important to me? (Yes, back to values again.) What was I really after? I wrestled with these questions before permitting myself to ink those numbers in. Having coaching clients wasn't all I was hoping for; I wanted serious clients who would value our work together and fully commit to doing the work between sessions. Often times clients will come to me with big desires to change their lives only to shy away or give up on the work needed to realize their goals. Coaching takes two. It's a partnership. Though we even have a written agreement that spells it out, when it comes to facing their fears not every client is willing, even if they think they are taking their very first steps.

I have read, and I have been advised that in order to have totally committed, successful clients, the amount you charge is important. It matters when a client sees a dollar figure that is significant— they don't want to waste it, which I believe psychologically compels them to try harder. Perhaps it's the bigger fear? No one wants to throw money down the proverbial drain. The money is important to me too. Not only does it allow me to support myself, it is important to me that my clients value my time and skill. I won't tell you what figure I decided to write next to "workshop" but to me it was significant. It represented the average per hour a client would pay, or a workshop attendee for that matter, which in turn represented what my new hourly fee for coaching would be. I didn't know exactly how I was going to arrive at that number, but I committed myself to it by writing it.

Fast forward six plus months later. Last night I was speaking with Jan about it. I had realized that my fee should be consistent with what my consulting firm charges so that I don't undermine their marketing. As we reviewed a recent project brief, did the math for the various components that make up a six-month coaching commitment, to my utter amazement it comes to EXACTLY that figure.

Now, let's be real, it didn't happen magically. As a coach, I am well aware of how this comes about in steps. What is different is that I didn't take steps. I named and wrote my number then promptly forgot about it. Thinking back from that moment until now, this stretch goal for me was the result of several factors: working with my own brilliant coach, working alongside several other experienced executive coaches who have advised me of industry norms and their own practices; and aligning myself with a highly reputable consulting firm that offers executive and individual coaching. Naming what I was aiming for however, has a way of calling it forward. So, the result is not only having committed clients and being able to fully support myself with my coaching practice, but now I also have several workshops coming up, the first scheduled to take place in less than a month. Am I nervous? Of course! I don't know if I will bomb or succeed, but I'm doing everything within my power to experience the latter. To ensure my success I have given this workshop for free to test it. I've practiced. I've tweaked. Now I'm going to let go of the result and focus on being present with my audience. If it bombs I will learn how to do it better, however, *what I won't do* is give up. It's on my list and I'm going to make it happen.

Another point in the how-in-the-hell-did-this-happen category, is discovering accidentally that I was harboring a self-limiting belief about the market. Until I had written a figure that would stretch my comfort, I had clearly underestimated what the market would pay (*expect to pay*). I was stuck in that limiting belief without knowing it.

Though I wasn't aware of it, and therefore didn't set out to overcome it, creating a bucket-list-worthy goal pulled me through it. It is worth noting that I am still waiting to see if my yearly number will be achieved. List items have rarely come about in the way I think they will, which makes it so much fun to see how it happens. To me, the number is not as important as the creativity it inspires as I think "outside the box" to attain it. It also stretches me to take risks.

Go ahead, I dare you, put a number on it.

CHAPTER TWELVE
Dream Bigger
But Please, Smell the Roses

Jeanne was silent for a moment as she thought. The question I had asked I assumed was pretty straight forward, but I have to remember that she goes deep. "What has been the result of the bucket list we created?" was all I asked. For Jeanne, her bucket list wasn't at all about doing extraordinary things, yet it wasn't limited to day-to-day experiences either. For her it was about living with purpose, finding meaning and feeling the peace of knowing that the way she is living will leave her without regrets.

Her answer was profoundly wise. "It's about living alongside death— not in a morbid way, but with an awareness of it, and the ability to let go all the time." She continued after a moment of silence. (I admit, she caught me off guard.) "To tolerate the fear of the end is the beginning of peace with how I'm living." At this point I choked up. I was so glad we were speaking over the phone where she couldn't see me. I didn't want her to be distracted by my reaction. A caring and sensitive person, Jeanne would be concerned at the affect her words were having on me.

Jeanne continued, "There is not a person walking on this earth who doesn't want to feel their life has purpose; to be living the values we hold important to us, to start at the beginning and move in the direction that belongs to you..." she trailed off. Overcome by the sudden realization she sighed. "I was working [on this] *forever* without knowing it. It was so helpful to know what's going on with me [feelings] and what's important to me [values] when something comes up." Getting real about how this plays out in her work, she explained. "For example, with my rentals. I now know that what's important is *relationship*: having a good relationship with the tenants *and* the service people. When there were issues, it used to feel like an intrusion. Now it's my life and I'm connecting my values [relationship] to my tenants. I don't hate what I'm doing anymore. Parts I even enjoy." This was a huge shift for her. At the beginning of every session she would need to clear the stress of managing her rentals, everything that was going wrong, the overwhelm of having to do it all, feeling that she had no choice. This did not at all play out as she expected. That Jeanne could find enjoyment, satisfaction, and meaning in her work was not only a surprise to both of us, but exceeded my hope for her.

She went on. "And 'travel buddy' . . ." We had identified that traveling would be much more fun for her with someone who also valued travel and who could be responsible for their own experience, yet someone whom she could connect with at points to share and enjoy a trip. "I'm very clear that I'll be doing a lot of traveling, but I'm not sure how it [finding a travel buddy] will unfold. Then she went ahead and told me exactly how it was unfolding. Glad, once again, that she couldn't see me; I was smiling.

"There are three people who have stepped forward to accompany me, one whom I met on this last trip who reached out to me after I got back. Then there's a woman from my creative community who asked me out of the blue about going on a retreat with her. I set an intention, then it comes in ways all its own."

Here's that serendipity that I was talking about at the beginning. It's one thing to identify what's important and name an expression of that, but from there you have to let go of how it will show up. Sometimes it looks very different than what you had in mind.

Jeanne began describing the Small, Medium, and Large categories of her list. "Boulders that have been in the way are starting to move, to lighten. It helped to clarify and cement my goals. It's a good way to solidify where you are and where you want to go, to develop the small experiences that get you to the big goals . . . it's so important for me to know the next right thing to do."

I concurred. "Yes, please, stop and smell the roses—that's what finding small ways to live your values is all about. It's about enjoying what is, and enjoying it right now." She whole-heartedly agreed.

Referring to us, she brought up a great point. "Working in collaboration with somebody who is enthusiastic about it, and about my progress was so important. It got me out of my head." After hearing this, I realize that the coaching relationship is special and can affect the results of both creating and living your bucket list. She said that she trusted me and how important that was to taking the risks she took to experience what she named. You may want to consider hiring a coach to take you through this. More importantly, a coach will stand by you and champion you as you take risks or make the effort required to realize the experiences on your list. If you choose to do this without the guidance of a professional coach, choose a partner who is also creating a bucket list; choose someone who can be excited with you, champion you when the going gets tough, and share their own experiences. Remember, these list items are not going to simply materialize because you've named it or visualized it. Living your values even as they are in your Small category, and reaching for a Large goal of experiencing something extraordinary takes courage, time, planning, saving or earning, and effort. It is so worth it, but it helps enormously to have someone "in it" with you.

Finally, Jeanne concluded, "the most important thing we did was to identify my top four values: FREEDOM, SECURITY, TRAVEL, and RELATIONSHIP. There is definitely a shift in how I'm going through my days. Now I'm so much calmer."

I wondered if Paul would reply to my email now that our coaching was complete. He's so disciplined about doing only what needs to get done that I imagined my email might be put aside until he had a moment to think about it (which may never happen). "Paul," I wrote, "what's changing for you now that we've created your bucket list?" Much to my amazement, he called.

Paul was short and to the point. "I am re-learning myself."

"How do you mean?" I wondered aloud. Paul has a tendency to make everything or nothing statements, put a thought in a box, check it off his list, and move on. I wanted to make sure that he saw what changes he had made in his life, what was working so that it sticks, and figure out what needed more attention.

"Well, it had been so long since I had thought about myself that I actually *forgot what I like*. Like playing music. Now I carry around this pocket-size trumpet, and when I have a moment, I play. It's also a way I now connect with my brother. That's our common interest." I could not for the life of me picture where he would be playing this pocket trumpet, but self-managing my urge to ask I pushed past the derailing question that was on the tip of my tongue.

One small homework item that I had added as an accountability for Paul was for him to keep a gratitude journal. I asked him to write three things he felt grateful for every day for a week; then to give each one a number from one to ten rating his level of gratitude. A week later he reported that he actually did it, and that it was easy. When we ended our sessions I had suggested that he continue. I tried not to sound shocked when he told me he had. Curious about what he felt and noticed, I asked, "What kinds of things have you been grateful for, and where on the scale did you rate them?" Surprisingly, his range went from six to nine, mostly eights, and every item he listed was from the bucket list we had created. Remember, Paul's list was full of simple, everyday things, like watching the birds, walking, and speaking with his girlfriend. While his life was full of international travel which would make many of us envious, what he was after was more satisfaction day to day. I also had the feeling that he wasn't getting as much enjoyment out of his positive experiences as he could, so the journaling and rating of each experience allowed him to sit with each memory and feel the positive feelings again. (What this NLP exercise does is retrain your brain to make the positive experiences stronger. It also served Paul to challenge his habitual negativity.)

Paul continued, "What I like about the journaling is that it makes me pay attention and feel grateful, instead of all these moments falling into a blurred memory." We had brainstormed his value expressions so that he could experience them many times a day. This dreaming small worked well for him. Let's face it, he was already living what you and I might consider the Large category. To create a way for him to remember to experience the value expressions that we had brainstormed, we built-in cues like eating lunch or walking in the door when he gets home from work to trigger his memory to do them. Finally, Paul concluded our brief conversation with, "I think I'm actually doing it" which is exactly what we were aiming for.

A few months after you've created your bucket list I wouldn't be surprised at all to hear that you've experienced most of it. That's the idea. That said, I know how you may have had to fight yourself, namely your saboteurs, for what you value. Just writing it down can bring up strong saboteur thoughts like, "this is selfish," "I'm never actually going to be able to do *that*," or "this is all *nonsense*," (perhaps you have a spouse or partner that's saying this!). Just know that whatever you've created on your bucket list is only the beginning of actually taking steps to live it; and living it is only the beginning of how you may start to experience life.

While that (in) in itself is a challenge, and the whole point of this book is to dream small so that you can make every day count, I'm now going to ask you to look at your Large category and stretch yourself to dream even bigger.

Remember, you can't hit what you don't aim for.

Reach for something that seems unlikely to happen; an audacious goal. Then test your idea against the Risk, Requirement, Realistic questions to see if it belongs in your Dream category. There is an important distinction I want to make here. When I challenge you to dream even bigger, I'm not asking you to put more into your Dream category. I'm asking you to think bigger, aim higher, hope for more in your Large category. These experiences I'm asking you to imagine, while they may be a stretch, are attainable.

Dream bigger. An easy way to do this is to combine several expression blocks into one experience as Paul did. For example, we have "reunion" in our Large category, along with Amazon Tree House. While for us it would be moving a mountain to bring all the kids and their partners to the Amazon, we could stretch ourselves with dreaming bigger about this "reunion." Even having a reunion with all our kids in the U.S. is a stretch, to have it at a tree house hotel would be extraordinary. It will take planning, consensus, money, time, effort, but I cannot imagine a more joyful experience. And, perhaps we can throw in a celebration of something. I will have to weigh it against the other Large items on our list and determine how much Jan and I want to make it happen. All I know is that now that I've imagined this, we can envision it, decide if we want to do it, and begin achieving it.

It's your life, you're in charge, and you have much to gain. Actually, those around you have much to gain too. When I'm living my values, I feel fulfilled, content, open-hearted and generous. I give more freely of my time and energy to those I love. After all, I know how important they are to my life. Having a self-giving pursuit is good for everyone, if you need an even stronger reason to create and live your list.

For all we know, we only have this one life to live. Dare yourself to live greatly. I promise, you won't be disappointed.

Appendix
How To
Your Quick Reference Guide

This section is for those of you who can't keep this all in your head while trying to picture what each step looks like. Perhaps some of you want to noodle ideas while you're sitting on a train or a bus heading to work. Please remember however, working large on a wall makes this whole process so much more effective and will be more fun too.

To expand and re-create your bucket list when you're ready to add new experiences, or to take one part of it and "drill down" here are the steps:

Steps	Exercise	Purpose
Step One	Peak experience memories	To identify at least three values or as many as six.
Step Two	Brainstorm expressions of each value	To know what they look like to you in the world or in your life.

Step Three	Narrow to a top three expressions per value	To choose only the epitome of your value expressions.
Step Four	Being, Place, Thing, or Activity	To group your expressions into building blocks.
Step Five	Small, Medium, and Large	Create your matrix with expressions down the left side, and sizes across the top. Brainstorm what each expression could look like in each category.
Step Six	Building blocks	Combine several to create bucket list-worthy experiences. Write Risk, Requirement, Realistic in the upper corner for a sanity check.

Step One Summary
Peak Experiences Exercise

1. Find a willing partner who won't judge or criticize you.
2. Explain what the three levels of listening are, and begin with your first memory, preferably from childhood.
3. Review the values your partner identified. Accept as is, or refine values by asking yourself if that is the essence of what was important. Group like values.

4. Next memory you recall should be from young adult years.
5. Finally, recall and share a recent peak experience memory (it can be from work too).
6. Decide which values you want to work with. Choose from three to six. Save the others for future exploration
7. Bask in the glow of being in your happy place ☺
8. If you're doing this as a couple, identify which values are the same for both of you. (If you can't find any, find a therapist or save for a good attorney!)

Step Two Summary

1. Brainstorm expressions of each value (Figure 1)
2. You can continue with the same partner or choose a new one.
3. Post large sheets on a wall, gather large color markers, one color for each value (color optional)
4. Set a timer for three minutes.

Go! (You can begin by sharing an embarrassing story or brainstorm something that doesn't matter in your life experiences like "paper." See how many expressions of paper you can name.) When you feel warmed up, silly, creative . . . go!

Here's a small sampling of our brainstormed value expressions lists:

ADVENTURE	IDEA REALIZATION	NATURE
Appalachian Trail	Legos	Beaches
Michelin Star Restaurants	Build a???	Trees
Sailing	Invention	Flowers

Amazon Tree House	Art	Fields/Meadows
Blue water	Garbage	Caves
Camping	Book	Redwoods
France	Conservation	Blue Water/Warm
Street Food	Women/Self-reliance	Stars
Iceland/Ice Hotel	Workshop	Picnic
Horseback Riding	Charity	Kayak
Greece	Family Business	Vineyards

Figure 1

Step Three Summary
Narrow to a Top Three Expressions of Each Value (Figure 2)

1. At the end of your brainstorming, have the same partner help you figure out which are the epitome expressions of each value. This sounds easier than it actually is. Some will repeat in other values lists, some will be similar, some will be close to what you meant but perhaps there's a word that comes closer.
2. Cross out the ridiculous ones. (Easy peasy.)
3. Pay attention to the ones that repeat or could repeat in some form in other categories. Here's where the color markers come in handy: put a check next to the expression that corresponds with another value. The expression may have repeated or another expression may have come close.
4. Look for expressions with several checks next to them. Those must be included somewhere, but not everywhere. Decide where they belong and eliminate the redundancies.
5. You should have three epitome expressions of each value.

6. Marvel at how your values look in real life. Oooh, ahhhh.

ADVENTURE	IDEA REALIZATION	NATURE
Appalachian Trail ✓	Legos	Beaches✓
Michelin Star Restaurants✓	Build a???✓✓✓	Trees✓
Sailing	Invention✓✓✓	Flowers✓
Amazon Tree House✓✓✓	Art✓	Fields/ Meadows✓✓
Blue water✓✓✓	Garbage	Caves✓✓✓
Camping✓✓	Book	Redwoods✓✓
France	Conservation✓✓✓	Blue Water/ Warm✓✓✓
Street Food	Women/ Self-reliance✓	Stars✓✓
Iceland/Ice Hotel✓✓	Workshop	Picnic
Horseback Riding	Charity	Kayak✓
Greece	Family Business	Vineyards

Figure 2

Step Four Summary
People (or Being), Place, Thing, or Activity

1. Have a look at your values expressions and make sure they are either nouns/proper nouns or verbs.

2. Organize your values expressions (on another sheet of paper or this gets confusing) into groups of People (or the broader category of Being to include spirit or, animal), Place, Thing, or Activity. You can have multiple of a group, or none for a group.
3. Stand back and admire your work ☺

Step Five Summary
Small, Medium, and Large: Create Your Matrix (Figure 3)

1. Move all your work sheets to another wall, but keep them handy. If you're starting this on another day, bring your values expressions brainstorming and grouping sheets with you. Post them on a wall where you can see them in case you need to remember what you meant.
2. Start fresh by posting three large sheets on the wall, slightly overlapping so that you have one big surface to work on.
3. Write your values across the very top of the sheet.
4. Write your overarching value(s) just below those, centered.
5. In the upper right corner write "Risk, Requirement, Realistic." This is your sanity check.
6. In groups (of three expressions each) write your People, Place, Thing or Activity groups. If you have multiple of any group, don't list them one right after the other or it becomes too big a chunk. It's important to your creativity.
7. Now create four columns by drawing a vertical line to delineate even spaces for each column going across your matrix.
8. At the top of those columns write "Small" (for the first column), "Medium" (for the second and so on), "Large," then "Dream"
9. Go get a refreshment. You're going to need energy.
10. Begin with your first expression and imagine what it could be in each "size." Move across each category taking one expression at a time. When you come up blank, skip it. You can return to it any time.

VALUES	NATURE, ADVENTURE, BEAUTY, CONNECTION, IDEA, CELEBRATION		(Risk, Reward, Requirement)
EXPRESSIONS	SMALL	MEDIUM	LARGE
Amazon Tree House	Camping	Tree House Hotel/ Texas, S.C.	Amazon!
Blue Water	Virtual/IMAX or 3D	Kayak on a U.S. Lake, Shore	Curacao, Mexico, Mediterranean
Ice Hotel	Poconos (Cabin)	Canadian "Bubble" Train	Iceland
Build	Project Home Philly	Habitat Out-of-State	Tiny Self-Sufficient Village
Invent	Workshop	Widget to Market	Write a Book
Conserve	Balcony Vegetable Garden	Restore a Historic Building	?
Redwoods	Arboretum, Fairmount Park	?	California And National Parks
Caves	PA	VA	Foreign
Flowers	Balcony Garden Longwood Gardens	A Bouquet 'Just Because'	Flower Fields/ Holland Sissinghurst Castle
Family/Friends	See Local Family/ Friends	All Kids Together	Distant Friends, Family Reunion
Spirit	Meditation, Yoga	Retreat	?
Animal	Puppy sit/The Seeing Eye	Wild Ponies (MD), Birds	Raise Another Puppy or Adopt/The Seeing Eye

Figure 2

This is a small sampling of our bucket list. It doesn't include the expressions of BEAUTY or CELEBRATION, but it's enough to give you the idea of how it will look when you're finished. You may also have a Dream column. We chose not to.

Step Six Summary
Building Blocks

1. Combine two or three to create a "10" experience.
2. "Do it. Do it now!"
3. Repeat as desired.

About the Author

Mare Rosenbaum is a certified professional co-active coach (CPCC, Coaches Training Institute) and in the process of international certification with the International Coaching Federation. She is also an associate at The Curci Group consultancy where she facilitates meetings and retreats, and supports leadership development for regional, national, and global clients. Mare is the founder and principal of Homeward Bound Relocation, LLC where she coaches global relocating executive families from Philadelphia's Fortune 500 Companies and consults on relocation and talent acquisition programs in companies of all sizes. In the field of publishing, she is formerly editor of the historic *True West Magazine* and a former feature writer for *Bucks County Town and Country Living*. She has two children who are grown and pursuing their own careers, and lives in Philadelphia with her partner Jan.